Denis Zekić

SOCIAL SELLING & MARKETING

LinkedIn MAGIC 5 FORMULA

A Step by Step Method for Generating Business Connections and High Value Sales Leads

First published in 2018

ISBN 978-1-98331-340-0

www.DenisZekic.com
www.magic5formula.com
info@deniszekic.com

Knowing is not enough; we must apply.
Being willing is not enough; we must do.

Leonardo da Vinci

CONTENTS

ABOUT THE AUTHOR

Denis Zekić, founder of CeeDoo.com is an award winning online specialist with years of experience in both Business-to-Consumer (B2C) and Business-to-Business (B2B) sales and marketing sectors. Denis' background stretches from SME to several multimillion turnover ecommerce and Digital marketing operations across UK, Europe and globally, including some market leading international organizations. Denis is also a keynote speaker and presents regularly at various industry events.

Denis' mission is to help businesses consider and adopt all aspects of modern sales and marketing methods, assist decision makers and their teams in joining forces to create value for their clients as well as their organizations.

Denis' company CeeDoo provides expert guidance and implementation of most effective Social Seles and Marketing solutions in the market with a guarantee to significantly enhance their client's brand presence, improve conversion rates and help build ever stronger community of loyal customers.

"In two years that we worked together, Denis took our business from 'just as' to being the industry leader!"

B. Smithers, Ashworth

"Denis was key in developing and making successful our online selling ... not just because he fully understands what needs to be done but also the way he worked with the sales teams..."

J. Hamilton, Tesla UK

FOREWORD

Over the last few months, I've had the chance to get in touch with some of the most connected and influential business people, key-note speakers, university professors and authors in the world. More importantly, I established a business connection with many of them and at the same time, have become part of their professional networks.

If it was not for LinkedIn, I would have never achieved those contacts, and remarkably – the process was relatively simple and straightforward.

The days when social channels were used for connecting only with people you know from the offline world is now over. Today, the platforms are so much more and evolving almost daily. In fact, Social Selling as a modern form of sales and marketing process is here to stay for the foreseeable future. Digital marketing is now the most cost-effective solution for attracting new audiences. Traditional marketing techniques will remain expensive and beyond reach for most, especially when using mass media such as TV, Radio, Press or Outdoor. Investing in online will continue to be a cheaper option and one which will give the best return. Once the right online channels are deployed, the appropriate tools used and relevant content produced, businesses and individuals involved will reap elevated sales and marketing results.

This book does not claim to have all the answers to the contemporary sales and marketing trends. The goal is to prompt those who are willing for themselves and their businesses, to adopt best practices of today's online world and which can ultimately help to ensure a prosperous future. I believe that all modern professionals and their teams must be able to find those appropriate solutions in an easy-to-follow and easy-to-implement format, saving them time and effort. To that end, I address those objectives in the text that follows.

Arrangement of the book

In the first part I elaborate on Social media as being more than just a platform for personal communication with friends and family. I see it as an essential tool for businesses, leaders, entrepreneurs and various other professionals who are trying to inform and provide products or services to their target markets. For some, the notion of Social Selling might be new so, in the first couple of chapters I will attempt to describe what does it mean and what is the significance in today's market landscape.

From there, the journey continues to comparisons between traditional way of customer engagement and new sales and marketing flows. Although there are many similarities, I will describe the fundamental differences in the process of searching for the right audience, the ways how to outreach to them, provide true value and start engaging. Once these steps are achieved and relationships created, the efforts of opportunity creation and selling will be that much easier. In its most basic form, the art of social selling is nothing more than real-time customer engagement through use of technology. There are however some basic rules that govern these new forms of interaction which will be covered in the second part of the book.

But what better platform can there be to use for the customer engagement than LinkedIn? With 550 million users, it is the most popular Social Media channel for professionals around the world.

And best of all – for the main par it is FREE!

To simplify the processes from the initial Goal Setting through Planning, Executing and ultimately Converting, I devized a proprietary solution – which has been well tried, tested and measured. This step-by-step, easy to follow methodology is my collection of Social Selling principles and best available Marketing practices for achieving measurable business success using mainly the power of LinkedIn.

I named it: **The Magic 5 Formula (M5F)**

The M5F consists of 5 grouped activities forming its core structure. The logic behind this is that by following an organized method in a consistent manner, the results will be more predictable and the process management easier while at the same time the overall success has been ensured. By making it all structured and easy to follow, M5F creates an ideal balance of what is essential to do regularly in a most effective balance between time required and results desired.

It gives me great joy to share with you this unique Social Media and LinkedIn methodology for generating high value business opportunities.

Denis Zekić

July 2018

INTRODUCTION

Daily, we face a flood of information. The scarcity called "attention" is only given to those most relevant, interesting and engaging; if you address your target audience through high-quality content, rather than with overly sales and advertising oriented messages, you are best positioned to win them over. Nothing is more important in business than creating those long-term relationships.

Competition today is as fierce as it has ever been. More than ever, lead generation has become a critical task for businesses looking to get ahead in their market. Lead generation is often identified as one of the most difficult challenges facing companies today, as confirmed by the Hubspot survey below.

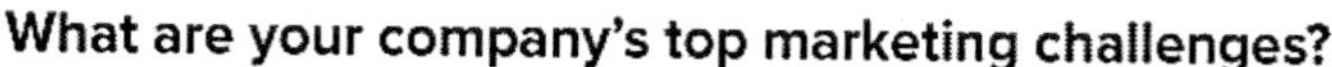

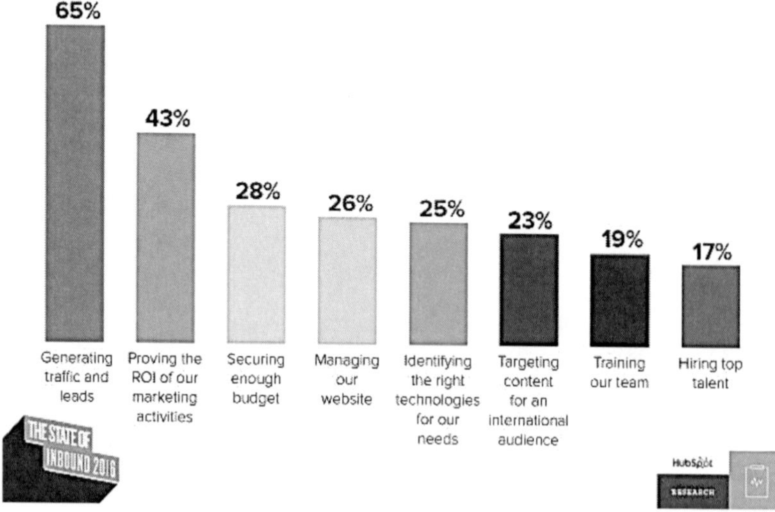

Source: www.hubshots.com/episode-52

What used to work is no longer considered effective. These days we need a broader approach. The internet and social media are the biggest differentiators that the industry disruptors and competitors are deploying to gain the advantage. And unless you have in place a solid Social Sales and Marketing strategy, your chances of succeeding in the socially connected online world are very slim.

Ignoring these latest trends and not implementing them is no longer an option. For economy and culture to progress, companies and individuals require an open mind and vision, courage and belief. In such a landscape, being cautious is a thing of the past. Now is the time to embrace the 'new,' and celebrate change.

Companies have two types of operations that are often viewed as conflicting; one focuses on the past and the other on the future. Traditional businesses are great at preserving value through an established model of capability and market recognition, but over time, these become dated, slow to change and eventually irrelevant. Start-ups, on the other hand, are great at spotting the market needs and driving a rapid change.

As little as 50 years ago, the life expectancy of Fortune 500 companies was around 75 years. Today, this figure is less than 15 years and is continuing to drop. Only 12% of the F500 companies from the mid-50s are still in existence.

There are many examples of companies who did not change with time and who are now a thing of the past.

Look into the B2C sector; Circuit City and Borders Books in the US for example, both closed their doors mainly due to Amazon. The latest victim to join the list is Toys R Us. Although they blame debt for their collapse, it must be said that they never adequately transformed themselves digitally, and so left it to their competitors to claim the online toys space. Toys R Us tried to fight Amazon's dominance by launching their own marketplace in the toys sector. But that strategy proved to be too little too late.

The Importance of Change

The question is not *if* disruption will come, but *when*. The important task is to prepare and shape your future, otherwise, the opportunity will be there for someone else to take from you.

There are three core business principles that all modern and successful organizations should uphold. These define the modern age and the way we produce, distribute, consume and communicate products, services or information. Let's look at them now:

High Purpose Through Customer Need

It is absolutely crucial to look through the 'customer's eyes,' and perceive our world from their POV in order to find out what they really need. Businesses must get on to the customer's level to establish what they feel, such as their wants, likes, dislikes, and emotions. We must organize our message around the customer, not around our own business or what we think the customer needs. The customer's first concern is not the product we sell, but how we can solve their problem and ease their pain. By putting ourselves in their shoes, we can get a better idea of what the customer wants and needs, and then figure out a way to solve that problem for them.

I'm not sure if you still remember your first mobile phone, but I do. It was the size of a house brick, and had none of the modern features, cameras, satnavs and so on… But today I must have it all in a pocket size device, preferably manufactured by a chosen brand. Don't you? Whether we admit it or not, we have been changed, and so has our customer… We have all been inspired and shown the future, our needs are transformed, the expectations amplified, our feelings tampered with…

Innovation and Change

Innovation and change are difficult to initiate and implement, most of the time they are risky and frightening. Change can be threatening for some because it involves moving away from the comfort zone into the unknown. But to move forward, innovation and change are the only option we have if we care about our customers and our brand. This means that the focus must always be on being original and on creating, instead of wasting time on replicating existing ideas.

Innovative businesses are characterized by:

- anticipating the market and customers' current and future needs and desires;
- making the future happen by providing solutions and delivering first-rate results;
- creating tribes of willing customers (think Apple's new product launch day queues) who listen, follow and absorb information about your products; and

- most importantly, creating hordes of ambassadors for the product who adopt and spread the word with enthusiasm on our behalf.

"Innovation distinguishes between a leader and a follower."
Steve Jobs

Internal Culture and Vision

Belief in the common good and forward motion is imperative. The desire to make something that matters pushes us forward for the better. Strong and developed leadership, clear vision and courage are essential elements in establishing a strong foundation for any modern and forward-thinking business. And it does not end there; it must be nurtured at all levels and ranks, at all times. Momentum is built over time and to create the ideal future, it must start with every individual action we take in the present.

The Importance of Innovation

Adapt or Else!

If anyone believes they are "too big to fail," they must think about brands like Kodak, Nokia or Blackberry. We are all familiar with their common and relatively recent story. During the mid-90s, Kodak was the fifth most valuable company in the world, employing 150,000 people globally. Fast-forward 15 years later, and it has gone through liquidation. But the fall of one giant saw the rise of another, which led Nokia to become the biggest digital camera manufacturer in the mid to late 2000s, holding a 50% global market share in the mobile phone industry. Then in 2007, a man in jeans walks up on stage and takes out of his back pocket a new device that will revolutionize the technology landscape and change the way we used technology forever. That man was Steve Jobs from Apple, and the device he introduced to us was the first iPhone. By 2012, Nokia's market share dropped to just 3.5 percent. History was repeating itself, and this time, it was Nokia that found itself at the sharp end of the sword. Similarly, in 2016, BlackBerry released a statement confirming that they would no longer be designing and manufacturing handsets.

The point is this: change is an inevitable fact of life. Not being able to adapt fast and at the right time is no longer an option for any business regardless of its size since. Disruptions can occur at any time, in any industry, sector or business. The task of today's business leaders is to act, prepare and shape their company's future, otherwise, someone else will.

SOCIAL SELLING AND MARKETING

In a perfect world, the well of quality leads would never run dry, leaving businesses with an endless stream of likely customers, some of whom would become loyal fans of your brand. However, in reality, we know that's far from the truth. For acquiring leads, every business worth its salt knows that high peaks and deep valleys are an unavoidable part of any brand's journey. The good news is that the game has changed for businesses. And if you play your cards right, one could say the game has considerably changed in their favor.

As all businesses (and as a result B2B relationships) move towards the digital arena, social media platforms have become a fundamental tool for marketing, sales, and building relationships. Amid all this digital transformation, social sales and marketing via digital media are putting traditional approaches under huge pressure. Keeping this significant change in mind, businesses must realign themselves towards a new sales and marketing model that helps them reach out to a larger audience.

For businesses in the B2B sphere, a social platform such as LinkedIn can be leveraged to help business owners, executives and entrepreneurs on their journey to find answers to the most pressing issues they face in an ever-changing business landscape. By positioning oneself as an authority in a specific niche and providing potential customers with useful information, brands can come across as being trustworthy, and generate more sales leads to grow their business. The interactions we have with potential customers really matter for building the trustworthy relationship.

The reason brands should focus on social selling on platforms such as LinkedIn is that selling is no longer a process... it's a journey. In this book, I will break down social sales and marketing sequence to show how brands can leverage this new art of generating sales leads, building the brand loyalty and ultimately reaching out their bottom line using the power of Social Media.

Whether businesses like it or not, the fact is that we are living in the era of digital interaction and social proof. Basically, this means that the function of a marketer and business developer now revolves around creating and nurturing online relationships long before any business deal can be closed.

While traditionally taking the time out to engage with potential customers who have not yet shown interest in your product or service would be labeled a waste of time, the tides have changed. Nowadays, it's all about having an active online presence and interaction with both the existing and potential customers.

It's no surprise therefore that according to the Sales Benchmark Index, nearly 98% of sales reps with 5000+ LinkedIn connections succeed in achieving their sales quota. The research indicates that businesses which interact with their customers can better steer the customer's decision in their favor.

What is Social Selling?

Social selling and marketing are all about leveraging a brand's social presence to find potential customers and build a loyal following. The technique enables businesses to generate better sales leads by targeting the right prospects, and, helps eliminate the need for cold calling a target audience for lead generation. By using social selling as part of a marketing strategy, brands can build and maintain relationships with their customers in an environment of trust.

We live in a digital age of communication spearheaded by social media. Keeping that simple fact in mind, it is up to the business to leverage their social networks such as LinkedIn to drive sales leads. What makes social selling an important part of sales generation is that social platforms such as Facebook, LinkedIn or Twitter can be tools to learn more about the potential customer's personality, their interests and the pain points they are looking to solve before any sales communication starts. In this way, the technique helps connect businesses with potential clients who are already engaged on social media platforms and are interested in the way your product or service can help them solve their problems.

Brands that leveraged their social networks found success and became known as early adopters. For instance, when Oracle's (ORCL) sales team was formed, many people thought of it as a lost cause, particularly since connecting face-to-face with the customer was valued more by the customers than receiving a phone call. While that is still true on occasions, the rise of the internet in the 90s soon changed that mindset. But, there was one difference. Back then, businesses that adopted the internet (email), which was considered the evolution of business, did not know what to do with it, with many business owners opting to print out their emails.

Fast forward to today, and no company can imagine functioning without the internet and email. Similarly, social selling is considered as the evolution of sales and marketing for our times. And it doesn't have to be an overly complicated process either, you only need to follow a proven model which I will cover later in the book. Once the methodology is adopted, the full glory of social selling will be witnessed in a joint outcome with your existing traditional sales and marketing process.

The importance of social media keeps growing. Businesses and marketers must buckle up for the times ahead. According to Brand Watch, 96% of people who discuss a brand online do not follow up with the brand's own user profile. This means that companies must be prepared to go the extra mile to follow and monitor even those unbranded conversations that your target demographic is engaged in. While it's important to know what your audience is saying about your brand on your social channels, being privy to their conversations relating to your brand on other social platforms and forums is key to best manage brand health.

The Benefits

Many companies are reluctant to embrace social media or are unsure of the benefits if they do. But once you realize that the sales and marketing teams are clearly communicating, the productivity of both teams is amplified. Rather than having to struggle for control, customer information management is synergized, leading to a better alignment of resources, and improved sales results. Social selling will have a significant impact on your business, but only when it's done the right way. Once social selling is successfully implemented across the board of your organization, the benefits will be profound.

A good social selling strategy can help you get across even the most complex of messages while creating an environment that engages the customer. Sticking to the old ways of getting in touch with customers and industry influencers won't cut it anymore. While remaining on the radar is a constant challenge for any business, regardless of its size, harnessing the power of social selling will lead to those benefits.

In LinkedIn 'State of the Sales 2017' report, they looked at the influence of social to sales efforts. It is apparent that top salespeople are much more active in adoption and use of social selling.

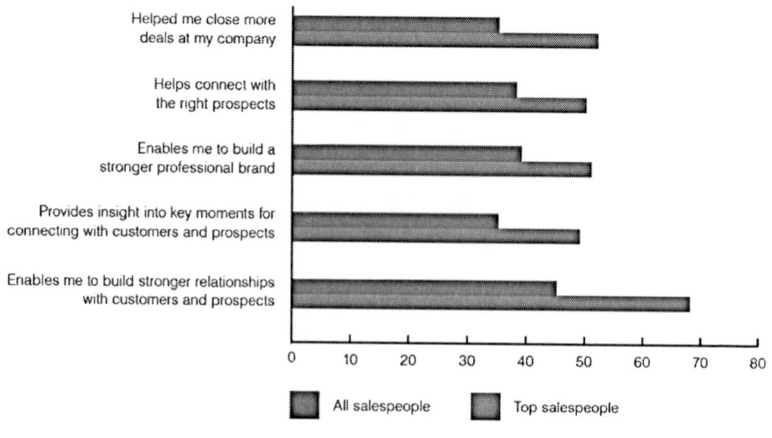

LinkedIn: 'State of the Sales 2017'

You Control the Message

The message or information communicated to customers can either make or break a brand. That's because in the digital realm two types of information exists. The first type is the information that's controlled by the individual business. This includes advertising, blogs, SEO, SEM, email marketing, and social media. The second type includes user reviews, forums, personal blogs, and feedback via your social media posts, and word of mouth. The second type of information is essential but not always easy to control. If not managed correctly, it can cause unimaginable damage to how a company is perceived, but if handled correctly it will become a crucial part of your brand's social existence.

According to a survey conducted by BrightLocal, more than half of US consumers (85% to be exact) feel that customer reviews play a big part in their decision to try out a product or service. That's because, while reading online reviews and interactions, consumers feel they are getting accurate information from their peers. While there's no way of guaranteeing you won't receive a single negative review from the customer, social media enables you to polish the image you wish to project, making sure you put your best foot forward. This ultimately encourages customers to write positive online reviews.

Social selling and marketing through LinkedIn, Facebook, Twitter, YouTube and other online media forums enable brands to contact their customers, interact with them and present a well-thought of and consistent brand message. But, again, brands must have a clear understanding and strategies for controlling these channels to adequately address the problems customers are looking to solve.

Who is Social Selling For?

Those who are still sitting on the fence for using social selling must realize the importance of connecting with their prospects at a personal level. The changing technology landscape continues to transform how we do everything, including buying. This means that in today's retail environment, selling is a sort of social process even if is conducted online. This also means that outdated marketing and selling techniques will not get you anywhere.

There are numerous examples of very successful brand awareness and customer base creation by Social Media in many sectors, but the rise of B2B Social Selling is reaching another level altogether.

In 2017, Deloitte Digital did a study with both B2B and B2C organizations to discover what they use social media for?

	% Using	B2B Product	B2B Services	B2C Product	B2C Services
Brand awareness and brand building	46.1%	45.3%	48.9%	45.6%	43.9%
Acquiring new customers	31.4%	27.0%	30.4%	36.8%	40.4%
Introducing new products and services	28.9%	29.9%	27.4%	35.1%	24.6%
Retaining current customer	28.4%	26.3%	24.4%	33.3%	38.6%
Brand promotions (e.g., contests, coupons)	28.4%	27.7%	27.4%	38.6%	22.8%
Improving employee engagement	20.1%	17.5%	23.0%	15.8%	24.6%
Marketing research	14.7%	12.4%	14.8%	17.5%	17.5%
Identifying new customer groups you currently don't target	13.7%	14.6%	14.1%	15.8%	8.8%
Identifying new product and service opportunities	11.1%	8.8%	14.8%	7.0%	12.3%
Improving current products or services	7.2%	6.6%	8.9%	5.3%	7.0%

Source: Deloitte Digital: 2017 CMO Survey

Technology is moving so fast these days that even the tactics considered new today will change and be outdated in the future. Those businesses that do not make use of social media through the sales funnel are at risk of losing everything. Not harnessing the power of social selling means to lose out on the profits and benefits attainable from it.

It is common for businesses to wait around and figure out how long it will take to seal the deal and leads to questions like, "why hasn't the prospect taken action?" The main issue with the traditional mode of selling was that it began on the wrong foot. Even if you are persistent with cold calling a prospect, psychologically they have set your business up is negative for chasing them about your product or service, or for showing up at their event. In Social Selling, the paradigm is reversed and your approach must demonstrate enough value for the customer to make a favorable decision.

With social selling, brands can shorten the sales cycle by sharing valuable information with the prospects beforehand. This adds to the value of your brand since you are perceived as an authority in your market niche.

It seems as if each year brings about new methodologies which sales teams are using to optimize their sales strategy. Regardless of the level of optimization a company is experimenting with, one thing is certain: no sales strategy can be complete without the proper integration of social selling techniques to drive sales. While platforms such as Facebook, Twitter and Instagram are all considered powerful tools in the marketer's arsenal, LinkedIn proved to be the leading platform for B2B social selling.

The good news is that even though social selling and marketing are not entirely new concept, there is still a huge level of opportunity left for all. This brings us to the question: who is social selling really for, and who can benefit from it the most? Also, how can companies utilize it to drive success?

Traditionally, the concept of gaining a competitive advantage over the competition which was also at the same time sustainable meant that companies built an imaginary fortress around their brand. These companies then defended the product or service they felt was a decent and therefore a defensible offering by locking horns with the client rather than making a sincere attempt to engage about the pressing service issues or worse, they simply ignored all the negative comments by staying away from any engagement on social media platforms. This also resulted in these brands losing all the positive comments and conversations. Through the years, businesses have cottoned onto the fact that if you want to get the customer's attention, you must try to start a conversation first. And nothing helps you do that better than social media.

A great example of the right approach to customer engagement was provided by Tesla CEO Elon Musk. On a Friday evening in August 2017, a Tesla customer tweeted this message:

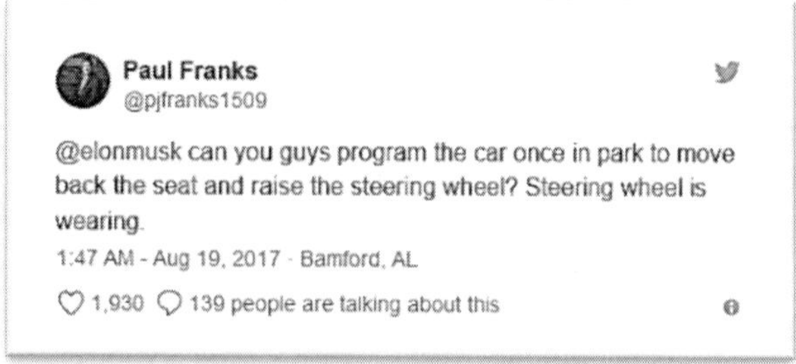

Less than half an hour later, the famous CEO replied with:

This is a fantastic proof how to use social media to listen and engage with the customer. If the CEO from one of the most innovative companies in the world can actively look for feedback and use it to improve his product, there is no reason why others cannot follow the same suit.

SALES AND MARKETING FLOW

Is your sales and marketing team dropping the ball when it comes to acquiring new clients?

You probably have tried out and are already using several iterations of the sales funnel model. A company with a clear lead flow structure sees fewer bottlenecks and achieves its sales targets. Once you have a clear structure, the next step becomes easier making sure each customer that walks through the door is steered through the sales process most efficiently.

It is not always the shortage of leads that companies struggle with, but one example of poor lead flow is that the marketing department will be getting an overflow of leads, which are then sent to the sales team. This may sound good on paper, but it ultimately means that the sales team is now stuck doing more work than they can handle. What makes it even worse for an organization is when there is no clear structure in place which can help separate the worm leads most likely to pay off from the ones that aren't. This way the sales team focuses on the wrong crowd and less valuable business deals that more often than not, grow cold in the end.

Research suggests that buyers are 50% more likely to go with the first person that sends them a response to their queries. This is important to the question of how quickly a business can respond to the potential customer and how likely the consumer is to move forward towards the next step. The average response time for an organization is 61 hours, for responding to their customers. An even more troubling statistic is that 47% of company leads receive no response. Remembering that, having a strong lead flow process can help identify bottlenecks and improve results.

The idea is to seize new opportunities and move them as quickly as you can through the sales funnel. More often than not, the sales team can get so caught up in the high number of sales leads the marketing teams managed to collect that they forget a very important factor of the funnel – the possibility of the lead dropping out before they can reach the end of the sales lifecycle. The question here is: how can companies take advantage of social selling to ensure that a sales opportunity is not lost while the lead is still going through the different phases of the sales cycle?

Remembering this, companies must know what strategy will help them jump on an opportunity when it presents itself. Without a doubt, those who are early adopters of the trend will reap the rewards enjoyed by early adopters of any trend.

Let's look at the rise of the internet. The first web browsers went online in the 90s. By the next year, just a meager million of the worldwide population were using the internet while the others stood in the sidelines watching and thinking. And just five years later, with an increase of 77 million users worldwide, the internet was no longer considered a passing fad but became a reality which most businesses had to cope with. Social selling can also be seen in the same light with the early adopters reaping the benefits, while others stand and watch. It doesn't take a rocket scientist to see that the field of marketing and sales is also going through a similar shift.

Traditional Outbound Marketing

Most businesses know about inbound marketing; it's the strategy of drawing customers in by creating interesting content for your website or social media posts. Most businesses are already using these techniques to get new customers. By contrast, outbound marketing is the more traditional strategy which deploys outreach forms of marketing methods to contact prospects to attract them towards the sales funnel.

No matter what your area of business or the industry you operate in, having the capability of bringing in new sales leads will be the lifeblood of your company. This is where methods such as account-based marketing as a form of outbound marketing come into play.

Traditional marketing techniques range from TV/radio advertising, telemarketing, cold calling, newspaper advertising, email marketing, direct mail, print advertising, to trade shows. Originally, marketing teams of several companies would combine all these resources to expertly generate sales leads for their businesses. Previously, for any business to get on the map, it was crucial to use this marketing tactic as part of the promotional strategy.

However, this approach is no longer considered the most efficient way of generating new sales leads, which begs the question, "*Should this marketing technique be abandoned altogether?*" The right answer is neither yes or no. One reason for this is that it still appeals to those generations, who have the habit of receiving a daily quota of ads via the TV, radio, and newsprint.

A good example of the shift in outbound advertising trends is provided by Adidas, the global sports shoes, clothing, and accessories brand. Their chief executive Kasper Rorsted said in an interview with CNBC in 2017 that the sports apparel brand has turned its back on TV advertising.

Rorsted explained that the company is looking to boost its e-commerce revenues from €1 billion ($1.06 billion) in 2016 to €4 billion ($4.25 billion) by 2020 — and Adidas is choosing digital channels to achieve these goals. He further told CNBC: "It's clear that the younger consumer engages with us predominantly over the mobile device. Digital engagement is key for us — you don't see any TV advertising anymore."

Traditional outbound marketing tactics are still proven to be effective in increasing B2B sales particularly if used alongside digital channels. Despite this, in recent years, we've seen that traditional outbound marketing has clashed with inbound marketing, with many businesses preferring to use the latter for lead generation.

A great example of using ad campaign related magazine articles can be given of an article written in Rolling Stone magazine on "The 25 boldest career moves in rock history." This article coincided with the famous Old Spice ad campaign featuring Jim Beam's "Bold Choices" commercial. Banners for the Jim Beam commercial were all over the place and appeared all over the article. Since the two were closely related to the entertainment industry, both were accepted by the masses since one was thoroughly entertaining while the Rolling Stone article was smart and informative. The trick here is to align your content with what's trending at the moment to attract an even larger audience. If your content is smart, informative and entertaining enough to garner the attention of the audience, they can create a positive association between your brand and any adjoining content which helps drive traffic.

Even a traditional outbound marketing campaign can be efficient in getting you the desired result if it is planned well and tailored to your business.

The key takeaway when using traditional outbound marketing tactics is that audiences no longer want to be bombarded by intrusive content that's not only annoying but uninteresting and a waste of time. Rather than just interrupting your audience's lives, give them something of value that's entertaining and informative. The goal is to get information from your customers in a non-invasive way and encourage them to think about your brand.

Online Inbound Marketing

If traditional outbound marketing is all about contacting a larger audience by any means necessary, then online inbound marketing is all about creating quality content able to attract the audience and influence their decision making at all levels of the sales cycle. However, this contemporary approach subsumes an ongoing process to nurture existing customers and attract new ones by appealing to their interests. For maximum publicity and lead generation, this strategy involves search engine optimization, social media marketing, blogging, email marketing, website, webinars, and podcasts.

B2B inbound marketing enables businesses to determine the success of their marketing campaigns through processing data. Thanks to technology, there's now a solution for all the common inbound marketing challenges faced by B2B companies.

In the hyper-connective world which we live in today, inbound marketing is viewed as a more appealing marketing approach for many businesses. Comparing the two methods, both have their advantages. While one strategy is useful for nurturing customers, the other is more useful in targeting choice leads.

Keeping this in mind, it's safe to say that both outbound and inbound marketing tactics should create a marketing strategy that's well-rounded and delivers results. Since we are moving towards a knowledge-driven society, with information just a click away, a synergy of both inbound and outbound marketing is the best formula for an effective lead generation. This will become important when we talk about LinkedIn social sales and marketing methods later in the book.

What's more, customers will always expect brands to establish credibility and build an engaging relationship with them, whether it's B2B, B2C, Software as a Service (SaaS) or ecommerce.

While the digital realm is chock full of many examples of strong B2B marketing content, here are few that will inspire you as you move forward with your own B2B inbound marketing campaigns. So, let's look at some.

Zendesk Engineering designs customer service software for their clients. But, while the company may have its expertise in providing software for customer service, it also has a whole chorus of high-skilled professionals who are the brains behind its software. The company was smart enough to realize that and to focus on an entire audience demographic who are in search of product insights and tips that are waiting to be tapped into. So, what does Zendesk do? It creates a content property that's entirely independent with the offsite insights on the technical side of the solutions.

Key Takeaway:

For B2B marketing, businesses must dig deeper to discover new and unique ways they can provide an even better service to their clients. So, if your service is to provide solutions to other businesses, you can enlighten your clients on your process. The things you've learned along the way, or the common mistakes and pitfalls you fell into yourself while coming up with your solution. Letting your customers know what you've learned along the way and how they can get there too is the value that customers look for. The right topic, when communicated in a casual, storytelling manner can do wonders in marketing content, which will without a doubt be viewed and appreciated.

Another example involves Deloitte, a professional services company that specializes in tech, auditing, consulting etc. The company operates in a cross-section of industries, and that knowledge has been leveraged by the company making it their major selling point. Deloitte has used their wealth of knowledge to create educational content such as the Deloitte University Press. Through this service, the company curates different pieces of targeted content that's helpful to those looking for knowledge and expertise in a particular field. Not only that, Deloitte also curates content in multiple formats including, blogs, podcasts, webcasts and in this way, offers a bit of everything to those who want to learn more about the industries they work in.

Key Takeaway:

Trying to create a wide variety of content will always be challenging. But, if you create content microsites similar to Deloitte University Press then you can keep the information organized and keep it from becoming unfocused. This is especially true if your company offers a number of specialties. Besides that, nothing is wrong with establishing your business as an authority in a particular niche, provided the content you offer is of value and better than that of your competitors.

Account Based Marketing

Rather than using a marketing strategy that's broadcasted to a large audience, consider focusing on a smaller target audience. Account-based marketing is a more strategic approach that focuses on single high-value accounts at a time. The audience that's targeted not just includes those identified as potential customers, but also those identified as high worth prospects from within a company.

Under the ABM strategy, all content is designed and sent through various strategic channels, specifically to those identified high-value prospects. It is used to create a more personalized approach towards a brand's marketing goals. This ensures that businesses only contact those leads that show the greatest potential of converting and being added to their customer base.

There are four key principles to an ABM strategy:

Identify

This starts with a business identifying the accounts that show the most promise of being interested in your brand and joining the cause, thereby becoming part of your bottom line. With B2B marketing, it's all about selecting a company based on its size, the number of employees it has, and the annual revenue it's able to generate. As part of an account-based marketing strategy, one can also use other data, such as buyer personas, to get a better understanding of the target audience.

Expand

Once the relationship has been established, businesses can create unique and company-specific content that's able to entice the potential buyer. During this stage, it is crucial for a business to use high-quality content that's customer focused and offers the audience value by addressing their challenges and answering their concerns. Engaging your audience in a way that's helpful to them will make a huge difference in their purchase decision. Here's where you must also identify the best channels to spread your message to your target audience.

Advocate

Now that you've been able to establish yourself as an authority in a specific niche, it's time to nurture your relationship with customers – they will become highly valued advocates for your brand.

Measure

Since you've identified and expanded your high-value target audience, and established a nurturing relationship with brand advocates, it's time to measure the fruits of your efforts. Statistics such as company growth and levels of engagement are just some of the analytics that can be used to find out what works and what doesn't.

Building an account-based marketing strategy will require patience and persistence. Whether you're using outbound, inbound or account-based marketing as part of your strategy, your promotional endeavors will take time to blossom and show impeccable results. You will be playing the waiting game regardless of which option you choose.

Later in the book, we will explain the way Social Sales and Marketing methods utilize this approach in a highly effective manner.

Sales Funneling

The sales process can be described as value-added steps carried out in a sequence, ultimately leading to a predetermined goal – the sale. The sales funnel or revenue funnel progression was first introduced by John Dewey in 1910. It is the process which potential customers are led through the stages of product or service purchasing. A sales funnel can be described as the breakdown of a would-be customer's journey. It can be broadly divided into several stages depending on the business model.

These include the awareness stage, interest stage, decision stage, action stage, re-evaluation stage, and repurchase stage. Here, we will take a quick look at the four most important stages of the sales funnel.

Awareness

During this initial stage, the potential customer becomes aware of their problem and the dire need for a solution. At this stage, they will realize there's an existing solution to that problem, which motivates them to visit your website.

Interest

At this stage, the potential customer starts to actively search for various solutions to their problem. This is the best time to attract a would-be customer with your product or service. This is where they are more likely to subscribe to your mailing list or follow your business on social media.

Decision

During this stage, they decide to use the solution you are offering via a product or service. They pay more attention to what exactly you are offering. The options and the packages are also evaluated during this process to reach a decision. During this stage, calls, webinars, and sales pages are used to entice customers with attractive sales offers.

Action

This is the final stage of the sales funnel and the place where the individual makes the leap from being a potential customer to becoming an actual customer and brand advocate. This is where the person will press the purchase button and transfer their money to your bank account.

Blogging, videos, Facebook Live, podcasts, social media posts, and lead magnets play a big part during each of these stages and can help brands build a demand for their product or service. While there can be additional stages, to avoid confusion, let's keep things simple. However, businesses should understand that additional stages exist.

It's safe to say that the sales funnel is where it all begins. But, the biggest mistake marketers and small businesses make is that they forget to align their marketing efforts with the structure of their respective sales funnel.

Marketing Automation

Providing the sales team with a steady flow of leads is the lifeblood of any business. But, finding quality leads takes weeks or even months. What this means is there's a lot of hand-holding involved, which is an additional reason to automate the process.

Nowadays, there's a growing number of tools and specialized approaches leveraged by businesses looking to use marketing automation to help drive their sales. But, what is it and how it is used? If you Google the term, the answer you get is it's a strategy that used automation to streamline and measure various workflows and marketing tasks. The data collected is then used to increase operating efficiency.

However, the secret sauce to marketing automation is personalization. This is a crucial factor regardless of the marketing tactics you use.

For instance, you might want to automate a drip-feed email campaign whenever someone converts on your landing page. This results in emails being sent to the customer at regular intervals until a particular action is triggered, which moves that customer forward towards the second stage of the sales cycle. In this way, a nurturing email campaign can prove effective as part of your marketing strategy. But, it will not have the same impact on the customer if the recipient feels that they are part of a mass mailout. Your customers must feel special as if an email is written just for them.

Second, the email you send out not only has to be interesting but also needs to be sent at just the right time, so the information sent to the potential customer is valued. To ensure your strategy succeeds, it must be integrated with an existing CRM (Customer Relationship Management) system, which also is tested and tweaked at regular intervals so you can keep the momentum going. Automation can help engage customers and it can also be used at different stages of the sales cycle. The typical areas where this shines are event marketing, referral schemes, lead generation and customer retention. It is also beneficial in cross-selling campaigns.

An automated email workflow can do wonders for lead generation from the time someone clicks on a link, subscribes to your newsletter, or is turned into an MQL (marketing qualified lead). And it doesn't end there. The level of engagement that marketing automation can create at the top of the sales cycle must be continued throughout the buyer's journey.

When using marketing automation, first, email your customers, highlighting your services and encouraging them to try your brand.

Once they've signed up to try out your product or service, send a second email a few days later to find out how the product or service is working for them. You can also use this email to highlight other features you think they will find helpful and interesting. Then follow up with a third email a few days later to

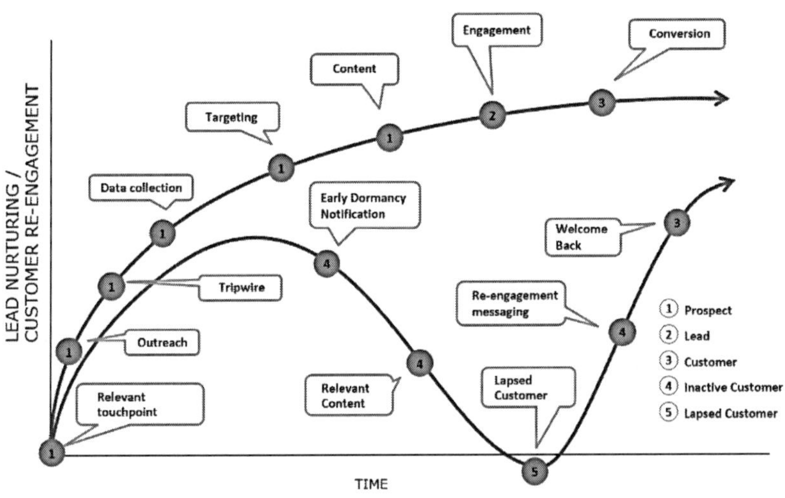

tell them ways in which other customers have used your product or service and benefitted from it.

Since it's always easy to retain the customers you already have, compared with going out in search of new customers, marketing automation can also retain your existing customers since it's unmatched in creating ongoing engagement. But, again, only workflows extremely personalized should be used for using automation to retain existing customers.

Paid Vs Organic Reach

As marketers get privy to the ways of fully utilizing social media tools and more specifically LinkedIn, one question that arises often has got to do with paid versus organic reach when it comes to marketing goals. To get an idea of how crucial a platform such as LinkedIn is to marketers, it has been estimated that up to 94% of B2B marketers use LinkedIn for distributing their content.

Paid search means paying for any social network (Facebook, Twitter, YouTube, etc.) to boost your reach helped by display ads, posts, videos and other content, which is charged on a CPM (cost-per-thousand) or CPC (cost-per-click) basis. Going the organic route means using free publishing tools of these social platforms to build a community where your brand and other members of your community can interact with each other by publishing posts (your brand), and (the audience) commenting on them.

Organic

Whether using paid or organic search while marketing on LinkedIn little changes. LinkedIn rolled out LinkedIn Pulse, its publishing platform back in 2014, and since then has witnessed steady growth of publications and professionals who use the platform to get their message across. Pulse has proven to be an excellent driver of traffic and revenue for countless B2B marketers using the platform to contact their audience in an organic way. It's ideal for those businesses looking to establish themselves as an authority in their niche while engaging their audience.

An estimated 130,000 posts are published by the million LinkedIn users each week, making it one of the best ways for marketers to contact their target audience – other businesses. Like publishing marketing content on other platforms, marketers use relevant industry keywords to make their content easy to search by those who are more likely to be interested in their products or services. To make sure your published content gets maximum exposure, marketers user hashtags (#) or sometimes the Twitter handle @LinkedInPulse to feature their content under one of the many content categories.

Paid

Just last year, LinkedIn introduced 'Matched Audience' a feature that allows marketers to use LinkedIn ads to email contacts who are non-responsive. While LinkedIn already offers users a way to conveniently target members based on their skill set, company or industry, the Matched Audience feature helps those marketers who want to contact people who they already know. The InMail paid feature is also another great way for marketers to reach out to their contacts in a more personalized and direct way than ever before.

The reason this feature is significant to marketers is that it is almost impossible for LinkedIn marketers to connect with each and every one of their LinkedIn contacts. With the InMail tool that's part of LinkedIn's Matched Audience feature, you will also find other features such as, 'Website Retargeting,' 'Contact

Targeting,' and 'Account Targeting,' which are useful and allow marketers to connect with their mailing contacts.

This book is largely focusing on organic LinkedIn lead generation, but to get more understanding how the paid advertising works head over to:

https://business.linkedin.com/marketing-solutions

SOCIAL INFLUENCING

The past decade has seen the internet gain a predominant position as a retail platform. This has helped generate a steady growth of the number of e-commerce sites competing for the customer's attention. The increase in e-commerce websites has had an impact on the online retail sector not only around the world but has also affected traditional brick and mortar retailers, encouraging both to create new marketing strategies to keep up with the demand and the competition.

At the same time, we see consumers really starting to embrace the possibilities of purchasing almost anything online, resulting in consumers nowadays spending more money when visiting online stories. With these developments, we are also witnessing a new form of marketing known as social influencing that's gaining traction in the digital sphere.

We are seeing more e-commerce retailers use plugins or features on their websites that enable consumers to interact and share useful information on the products or services they are purchasing online. The element of social influencing provides the consumer with an opportunity to gauge a product or service based on the views and opinions of other consumers, mostly, and this trend seems to have become the norm.

The constant sharing of information regarding products or services found online is taken a step further by online retailers encouraging their customers to pay in alternative currencies with a simple click of the button such as pay per tweet or pay per like options growing in popularity. Besides that, the consumer also has the option of leaving a review, rating the product or service and giving their own personal feedback about their latest purchase for all to see.

The modern consumer is in constant contact with the influence of not only their friends and peers, but also companies, and even strangers. Social influence has evolved into a highly effective strategy that's used to pique the interest of consumers. And this is not limited to B2C, but also B2B sales, because in both cases, the news is driven by useful content and authority in a particular niche.

Remember when we mentioned that the modern consumer is in constant contact with influencers who are not just other customers, but business owners who have become privy to the real power of a social media influencer. These aren't just average Joes with an opinion, but marketers and business owners who have promoted their products. The reason for this change is that the lines between business and real life are blurring now more than ever, which is why we see a growing number of business owners wanting to get in on the action of social influencing.

Take the example of Motorola; when they launched Moto Mods and Moto Z family their goal was to establish the brand as a new standard in the smartphone market. They realized that they can effectively tap into the Social Media market reach via the influencer marketing methods to promote the new product. They chose a dozen of YouTube influencers for the job, with each posting videos about new Motorola. Meredith Foster, a YouTube vlogger with around 5 million followers published engaging videos with exciting stories about Moto Mods. The video attracted over 500k views and provided Motorola with an effective way to communicate with the target audience.

For businesses to take on the role of social influencing makes sense since you get to spell out how you live and invite others to take a peak before hiring/buying a service/product. Here, we will explore the traits that make an influencer and how business owners can transition to influencer marketing.

Listening

A large part of becoming a social influencer is listening. This begs the question, "How does one go about social listening?"

In simple terms, this means analyzing data about your target demographic. It includes what the customer is saying about your product or service. What the customer thinks about your competitors and the niche in general when they use social platforms.

Entrepreneurs who know the basics of marketing know the importance of content. Before you begin, do your research on other brands and influencers to see what strategies they use to attract customers. By "listening" first and then creating can deliver a high level of engagement. This process is easier said than done, but with the right social listening tools, any marketer can get the information they need.

Using basic metrics on engagement levels you can gauge the content you create for various social platforms. Key metrics such as the number of views, shares, likes, pins, retweets and any other action that your posts can achieve will prove that your followers are actually engaged with the content you're putting out.

For those just starting a new business, it makes more sense to look out at other influencers. Adopting the best practice from others and stitching together your own marketing strategy can help you save big while getting the traction you need for your website.

Listening to the concerns of your audience, then using the right metrics to measure engagement rate and velocity will give you a clear picture of which type of content is performing better, and on which channels.

Set A Clear Goal

The first thing you must focus on before measuring anything is to have a clear idea of what you want to achieve with your marketing strategy. Focus on those goals that can be measured by metrics, while trying out ideas that are non-specific and cannot be measured. So, what do you want to achieve? Do you want to increase your Twitter following by 30% by the year's end, or are you aiming to contact a few thousand consumers via Facebook? Also, you would want to be realistic while setting your goals. If you are still confused about how to go about a DIY influencer marketing strategy then simply follow the S.M.A.R.T way, as in, think of a goal that's Specific, Measurable, Attainable, Realistic and has a Timeframe.

Empathy

The role of a good marketer is to move opinion, to be influential, not only to the customer but to the potential influencer. This makes the principle of empathy increasingly valuable if you're looking to go the route of influencer marketing. If so, it is your responsibility as an entrepreneur/business owner to create an environment where your customers and the potential clients in your niche will be prepared to change their opinion regarding your product or service. This is achieved by sprinkling your content with a bit of empathy. As a marketer looking to fill the role of an influencer, sure you want your audience to hear your story and understand what you are trying to say. But, they must trust you first. The following are important lessons I learned from business owners who juggle the role of influencer and entrepreneur.

"I Walk the Line"

While social marketing can take on many forms, at the end of the day, you can't just expect to slap "influencer" before your designation and expect people to follow you, or your sales to go through the roof just because you also own the business. It's all about having a great product with an inspiring story that will reach the heart of the consumer. One of the best stories of entrepreneurs who walk the fine line between influencer and business owner can be given of Michelle Phan and her YouTube makeup tutorial channel. Back in 2013, Phan was accused by her fans of selling out when she launched a new collection of products in partnership with L'Oréal cosmetics. The only problem was, the cosmetics were $50 a pop, something that didn't go well with her fans. This showcased Phan's disconnect with her audience and severed the empathetic link between her and her followers. So, now you know the power that empathy yields.

Influencers Care About Their Content and Their Readers

OK, that was a mouthful of a heading, but nearly 35% of online consumers who follow influencers admit to being more engaged because of their high-quality content.

So, what's the meaning of "high-quality content?" It doesn't really matter if you use long-form blogs and articles that go up to 5k words, or short-form content that's just a few hundred words per topic, it's the quality of that content that really matters. Those who have been in the game for a while as influencers know all too well that their audience comes back for more because they can create content that's of value to the reader, and are, therefore, turned to for advice because they are viewed as an authority on a niche.

The good news is that, as an entrepreneur who's just dipped your toes into an influencer marketing, you will have quite a few experiences to share or valuable inside information that only someone who's in the business circle would know. If you want to be a powerful thought leader while wearing the hat of a business owner, you must care about the content you create and those who read it. Remember, it's not about you or what you can do for your audience, it's about connecting with the reader to show you understand what they are going through and want to offer a solution.

Celebrities are Human Too!

Remember when Oprah plugged a Surface (Microsoft) while using an iPad (Apple)? Not very smart. But hey, even Oprah can make an honest mistake.

Speaking of honesty, here's another great example that entrepreneurs who want to pick up the mantle of influencer can use.

In May 2017, the popular American TV host Jimmy Kimmel used his opening monologue to share a tear-jerking story of the birth of his son. While it was expected to be a normal delivery, the baby had to be transferred to a Children's Hospital due to a complication. During his monologue, Kimmel praised the doctors for saving his son's life and praised the work of the doctors of that hospital in Los Angeles. In the next few days, the Children's Hospital at Los Angeles not only noticed a significant spike in their followers on Facebook but also received thousands of dollars in donations. The hospital also received many phone calls from the corporate sector inspired by their work and wanted to give donations in honor of Kimmel's son.

The honest monologue indirectly made Kimmel an unexpected spokesperson for the hospital. While having access to the platform of his own show was a factor, the power of Kimmel's story was able to move millions. In the same way, the power of honesty and of the ability to connect with an audience is a crucial weapon in the arsenal of any influencer.

Rapport

To cultivate trust between your brand and customers you must build rapport with the audience. This is where employee-education also comes in. Why you may ask? Even for an entrepreneur who wants to step into the shoes of an influencer for their brand, you can't do it all by yourself, at least not usually. Businesses with employees must cultivate a culture that helps build trust. The best way of doing that is by getting your employees involved with connecting with your customers. Rather than blasting their rehearsed sales pitch, business owners must teach their employees how to start and maintain meaningful conversations with the customers. Business owners can also get their employees to posting relevant content at specific times to add value to your brand. Using social mediums such as Facebook, Twitter or LinkedIn businesses can get closer to their audience by grabbing their attention with valuable content. Particularly important is to ask your employees to like and comment on pieces of content you put out.

Some statistics from LinkedIn show that 30% of all social traffic to corporate websites is driven by 3% of the company's employees. By using a simple math, you can predict the effect of engaging the whole business in promoting the organization through social media.

Be Passionate About Your Brand

If you want to act as an influencer for your brand you need to be passionate about what you've created, whether it's a product or a blog. That passion will show whenever you are having a conversation with your customer. And if you manage to pass the same passion to your employees, the customer will almost certainly recognize it.

Address Issues Right Away

As a spokesperson for your brand, you will need to address any issues as soon as they arise. The customer might be experiencing issues with your brand or may have a complaints or suggestion. Whenever a customer comes to you with a problem, by reaching out on your website or social media, it is up to you to try to resolve that problem as soon as you can. Not only will this show that you respect your customers, but also that you care about your customers. When dealing with a dissatisfied customer, regardless of whose fault it is, always be polite. Try to address the issue as it is and make it clear to them that you're going to do everything possible to make sure the issue doesn't arise again.

There are occasions where negative comments are of such nature that they are not suitable for public display, or sometimes specifically created to damage your reputation. With most Social Media including LinkedIn, you have an option to block the person who made the comment. Bear in mind, that if you block the person first – their comment will stay live without you being able to see it. So, the best practice is to delete the message and then block the person. If you only do the first, then you may leave yourself open to even higher degree of abuse and foul content.

Sure, you're passionate about your brand. Every entrepreneur is. But, it's not something you'd want to be accused of when trying to build rapport with your customers. All too often, entrepreneurs who wear too many hats end up being too aggressive when pushing a new product or interacting with their customers. Planning in advance with the use of automation tools is a great way to make sure you didn't buzz the same client twice in the same day.

Influence

Whenever a customer enters an online retailer, they are not only met with information regarding the product or service they want to purchase but also information created by other customers. Usually, this information is shared on the social media pages in the form of reviews. This is known as 'real opinion information.'

However, there is another form of opinion information that's not generated by real customers, but the brand itself with the purpose of endorsing a product or service. A good entrepreneur who wishes to also be an influencer for their brand needs to have the following traits.

Relevance

An authoritative influencer will always occupy a clearly defined niche and will always stay on topic. Relevance matters for influencing others since there is a direct correlation between the relevance of information and audience engagement. The more relevant your content, the more comments, shares and likes it can generate, and that's a good thing for promoting your brand.

Consistency

To build influence in the digital ecosystem, you must keep at it. That is what influencers do and are good at. A successful entrepreneur who wants to influence others will always maintain a level of effort that will allow them to publish quality content on a regular basis. Thought leaders who have been in the game for a while know all too well the importance of staying in the game and feeding the audience with fresh content and so must you.

Originality

Always offer something the audience won't find any place else. Influencers know the importance of expanding their content beyond what's traditionally accepted and creating content such as industry insights or insider tips on a product or service that's informative and unique. Since business owners will be operating in a particular niche, it's time to use their experience and knowledge and share the love.

Authenticity

Having years of experience in a particular niche will validate your thought leadership. This is because those following you will know that your information is based on truth. Business leaders able to share their personality, differentiate themselves from the rest, they appear more authentic when trying to influence others.

Trust

One reason why an audience will look to you for information is that they trust the information you must offer. While the audience will always follow an influencer who they can trust, it pays to be transparent. Always be honest with the information you provide. There's nothing wrong with blowing your own trumpet, as long as the music you create is bearable. Being transparent and not trying to pose as someone you are not will help to secure the trust of your audience.

Participation

Again, grabbing the attention of your audience can be exhausting. But, that hasn't stopped social media from becoming the top marketing tactic used by many. As consumers look to key influencers for social proof, entrepreneurs and business owners can also develop their own influencer marketing strategy and establish themselves as an authority in their niche.

Community Engagement

Using content to create awareness for your brand is another important factor in social marketing. This can be achieved through contests, campaigns, and vouchers to trigger a specific response from your targeted audience.

Be Social

There is no point in having a presence on social media and a fancy Business page on LinkedIn if the last blog you posted was three years ago. Being social means having your finger on the pulse at all times. As an entrepreneur who wants to engage their audience, it's up to you to start a conversation by consistently creating great content for your social media posts.

If you get a strongly worded comment from a customer, help drive the conversation by asking your audience to share their opinions.

Sales

If you've got a product or service to sell (and you probably do), teach your sales team to be friendly with customers, and always share quality information that will help solve their problem. No one said taking the DIY approach to social marketing would be easy, but with the right strategy and positive mindset, anything is possible.

You Don't Need to Go at it Alone

When the going gets tough, you might need some help. Besides, four heads are better than one as they say. For participating in social sales and marketing there are two strategies businesses can take advantage of:

- Earned Influencer Marketing

This can be achieved by developing organic relationships with key market leaders. Earned Influencer Marketing is useful for individuals or start-ups to increase their professional growth.

- Paid Influencer Marketing

This strategy involves businesses hiring key influencers to participate in various marketing campaigns. This can be with testimonials, sponsorships, and pre-roll advertisements. The audience size and reach of the influencer will be the main determining factor in the budget for paid influencer marketing.

To succeed while participating in an influencer marketing campaign, marketers and businesses must pinpoint key metrics, and examine the data, avoid data overload, have an organized approach to reviewing and analyzing data. Marketers also must be focused on marketing attribution. Since influencer marketing is here to stay, it is up to businesses to develop long-term strategies to analyze data and prove ROI.

GETTING SOCIAL WITH YOUR TARGET AUDIENCE

Social selling, which literally means the act of developing relationships as part of the sales process is as old as the human race. By nature, sales is a unique human activity at its core. The existence of bartering is probably as old as trade itself, going back to the earliest days of human existence. Building relationship with key people in goods exchange must have always been an important element of trade, especially important when long journeys across land and sea were required.

This person-to-person contact built strong relations, developed confidence on the sides of the buyer and seller, and with something as symbolic as a handshake, salespeople would put their reputations on the line for their product or service. This evolved into modern telemarketing call centers and entire phone banks which leveraged the ability to connect with customers at a scale unheard of just a short time earlier.

Come 2018, social selling is in vogue more than ever before thanks to technology and social media platforms such as LinkedIn's Sales Navigator. This has provided B2B marketers with a leaner approach to networking that wasn't possible before and goes far beyond the traditional meet-ups and marketing summits. It's no wonder that a social media channel such as LinkedIn is used by 61% of B2B marketers to increase their lead generation.

According to estimates, the number of social media users will be just shy of 3 billion by 2020, so it doesn't take a genius to see that social selling and marketing are more effective than cold-calling a thousand people or blasting out thousands of random emails. With growing competition, businesses must leverage their brand and fill their pipeline with the right people. This can only be achieved by gaining insights into one's target audience and building stronger relationships.

While social selling won't be your only game, it's crucial for it to be part of your brand's strategy to achieve success. Social selling can be viewed as the ultimate equalizer that allows even small companies to compete with large organizations.

The evidence is stacked: using archaic methods of marketing is no longer viable for any business that wants to grow. That said, today's consumers are smarter and self-educating, they are also tech-savvy and social, which means they are spending more time online, taking part in online communities and getting to know their brands. However, interpreting your social selling data is just as crucial as using social selling as a marketing strategy.

The smart marketer knows all too well and does not for a second assume that by simply using social selling they will see their numbers rise. The truth is, any social selling efforts are only as good as the person using them. So, to convert more connections into leads and those into sales, a marketer must first identify their target audience and curate content that resonates with that audience, while still being infallible in the art of subtlety.

Make Mistakes, But Make Them Count

Making mistakes is not bad. It allows us to learn, and that can be a wonderful thing. When it comes to social selling, it is not enough to just learn from your mistakes, you must try to correct those mistakes as fast as you can. One of the many factors that separate social selling from other forms of marketing is that it provides businesses with an opportunity to engage with the customer in real time.

This allows businesses to interact with their customers on a scale that never existed before. This means that both the good and bad are equally amplified across the internet, which can potentially harm your brand's image. This means when you make a mistake (and you will), you must take every possible step to correct it fast and put measures in place to you never make the same mistakes again.

Measure Your Success

LinkedIn offers grades to those brands that use its platform for social selling. There are four criteria that go into that rating, known as the Social Selling Index (SSI);

- Amount of content shared by a marketer/brand
- Number of connections a marketer/brand has with their target demographic
- How often marketers/brands interact with others
- How often marketers/brands slick on their feed insights

To check your SSI, go to *www.linkedin.com/sales/ssi*

Businesses using social selling can get their team excited with their SSI score by carrying out a team-wide competition of who can raise their SSI score, which will have a positive impact on your sales targets and will lead to better brand exposure. All the more, it's the reason your brand needs a company-wide social networking engagement strategy.

Choose the Right Time

One problem that B2B marketers face while using LinkedIn is finding out the right time to contact their target audience. LinkedIn takes care of that with its 'Connections in the News' tool, which was previously acquired by LinkedIn in 2014. This allows users to congratulate connections on their milestones. It allows B2B marketers to revive previous conversations by keeping interactions focused on the customer's success. It also allows B2B marketers to reach out to businesses when looking to reinvest by making purchases. Besides that, by showing interest in the success of your prospective customer, you gain more trust, which is a big plus for any relationship.

One mistake that many B2B marketers using LinkedIn often make is they take the meaning of "patience" to a whole new level. We've already identified today's customer as being smart and tech-savvy. This means, for the most part, buyers have gone through three-quarters of the sales process before they even hear you speak. Your prospects do not need you to give them information on your products or solutions since they've probably already "Googled it." They've discovered your brand, reached out to online communicates for suggestions and have read the reviews. So, if you are on the shortlist, it's time to act, and act fast!

One reason why social selling clicks is that it allows marketers to shorten the time it takes in connecting with prospects and closing the deal.

By using the Five Step Methodology and some common social media principles, B2B professionals can leverage LinkedIn as an easy and effective way to create a network for business development on a global scale.

Savvy marketers use LinkedIn to spot, develop, and sell to prospective customers in a manner that's non-salesy and effective. For marketing a brand, social selling is a win-win. According to Social Media Examiner, more than 80% of B2B marketers are looking forward to using LinkedIn more than they already do. While there's no quick fix to building relationships on LinkedIn, the second part of this book will teach you how to do exactly that in a serious of tested and proven steps.

FUNDAMENTALS OF LINKEDIN

Setting the Objectives

There are several objectives for businesses and individuals using LinkedIn, but before we delve into those, let's look at the most common questions people have in relation to signing up for an account.

Why do I need LinkedIn account?

Your industry and customers are changing, and so should you. If not already, taking social media seriously should be one of your major objectives. Think of LinkedIn as the biggest business networking event there is, regardless of what your business or personal goals are. It's all there for you: your professional connections and business partners, customers - existing and potential, their stories and biographies, the tools and know-how to engage and create value for all.

You've heard the saying that in business "It's Not What You Know, It's Who You Know." I don't intend to debate this aphorism, but it is a well-documented fact that reaching business success is impossible in isolation. Having the right contacts, conducting the right conversation with right people, at the right time and place will lead to better and faster business success. Having a professional network is one of the most important business imperatives, and what a better platform for that, then LinkedIn.

What can LinkedIn do for me?

The LinkedIn user base can be divided into five main categories. Depending on which career or business development phase you are at, at least one of the following will fit your bill:

- Career progression/new job
- To inform or Be informed
- Staying in touch with business contacts
- Meeting new professionals/do networking
- Generating Leads

Does LinkedIn work?

Let the figures do the talking:

- There are over 550 million LinkedIn users globally
- 40% of members, use LinkedIn daily
- Presence in 200 countries
- 80% of all B2B social Leads come from LinkedIn
- 93% of B2B marketers consider LinkedIn to be the most effective site for lead generation
- 50% of LinkedIn members report they are more likely to buy from a company they engage with on LinkedIn

What are my goals?

Sales and marketing can both use social media to discover and influence any potential buyer at any point in their journey.

Your goals can be multiple but will always include creating and building relationships. You must identify problems and pain points in a prospect's organization, then share content through meaningful engagement. By participating in such communication, you will demonstrate your expertise and prove the value.

What do others use Social Media for?

"The CMO Guide to LinkedIn" research which LinkedIn published in 2017 shows that 82% of consumers are more likely to trust a company whose CEO and leadership team engage on social media, while 77% are more likely to buy from such a company.

When top U.S. marketers at for-profit companies were asked how and why do they use social media, they indicated that Brand Awareness and Customer Acquisition were their main objectives. This chart clearly supports Social Sales and Marketing being one of the major shifts in business development strategies for modern organizations.

	% Using	B2B Product	B2B Services	B2C Product	B2C Services
Brand awareness and brand building	46.1%	45.3%	48.9%	45.6%	43.9%
Acquiring new customers	31.4%	27.0%	30.4%	36.8%	40.4%
Introducing new products and services	28.9%	29.9%	27.4%	35.1%	24.6%
Retaining current customer	28.4%	26.3%	24.4%	33.3%	38.6%
Brand promotions (e.g., contests, coupons)	28.4%	27.7%	27.4%	38.6%	22.8%
Improving employee engagement	20.1%	17.5%	23.0%	15.8%	24.6%
Marketing research	14.7%	12.4%	14.8%	17.5%	17.5%
Identifying new customer groups you currently don't target	13.7%	14.6%	14.1%	15.8%	8.8%
Identifying new product and service opportunities	11.1%	8.8%	14.8%	7.0%	12.3%
Improving current products or services	7.2%	6.6%	8.9%	5.3%	7.0%

Source: Deloitte CMO Survey and Digital Report 2017

How can I use LinkedIn to achieve my goals?

As seen in the previous reports, it is a well-accepted fact that building reputation, authority and/or personal brand is impossible without active participation on Social Media, with LinkedIn taking the lead position when it comes to B2B sales targeting and lead generation.

Additionally, helping others to solve their pressing problems and guide them to reach goals on their own quest for personal, professional or business success should be your primary and the true objective to aim at. Anyone who helps others will be rewarded eventually and ensure a strong business existence with a guaranteed financial return.

Unless you're already using LinkedIn as the main channel to achieve your business goals, I suggest you make a swift move to doing so.

Creating the Plan

Studies show that the average B2B buying process in the corporate sector has 7 decision makers involved. To make sure you are creating a focused campaign for reaching the right decision makers, you must come up with a detailed plan. Let's see what first steps you must take to leverage the network and engage with your contacts.

Optimizing your LinkedIn Account

This is exactly where many go wrong, and yet is one of the most obvious things to do. Think about the rollout of a cohesive sales and marketing plan. What do you think should be the prerequisite to make it work? Your profile, for sure!

The first thing any potential contacts and the future client will check out is your profile. First impressions count, so for someone coming across your business for the first time, they will seek to build a full picture of your professional credibility. They will examine your personal and business branding with any industry relevant content as a tangible evidence of your authority.

The second part of this book is dedicated to LinkedIn account setup, so feel free to jump over to the section-by-section guide to learn more about how to create the winning LinkedIn profile.

The plan

Organizing the sales and marketing teams around social selling will lead to a new way of operating. A modern approach to generating and following up on leads will inevitably be a challenging process, particularly if traditional methods are confronted and pushed aside.

It's not only with Social Selling, but any change is painful. Those who persevere will reap the benefits. Evidence shows that social selling transformation typically increases conversion rates by 20% to 50%, while in some instances, even higher.

The starting point should include planning, and these are some of the main headings to cover:

Defining the Objective:

- What are your expectations?
- What would you like to achieve?

- Does it meet the company overall plan?
- Are your objectives measurable?

Target Market

- Who is your customer?
- What is the size of your target market?
- How to identify them?
- Likelihood of their positive response?

The process

- What will be the process?
- Who in your organization will be involved?
- How much of it will be automated?
- Draw a Step-by-step flaw map
- Make sure it is optimized and no questions left unattained
- Define timescales and deadlines

Setting the KPIs

No matter how sound your plan and execution are likely to be, the importance of setting your Key Performance Indicators (KPIs) is of make-or-break importance. You must understand whether you are achieving strategic goals or failing. Do you have to react and adjust, or push forward? Without tangible measurement, none of these will be clear and may jeopardize the whole process and even more importantly, you cannot quantify the value delivered to your customer.

Spend some time to determine which KPIs you should be tracking bearing in mind that the process of Social Sales & Marketing does not reside in one or two departments. All teams within the organization should play a role in delivering value.

Synchronizing all departments to work collectively on these objectives, on the other hand, can be very challenging without a metric which focuses on a common goal.

In recent years, Silicon Valley companies spearheaded by Sean Ellis from growthhackers.com have been adopting "The North Star Metric" (NSM) method by which the whole organization focuses on a single metric that best measures the core product value delivered to customers.

As an example, numbers like page views, visits, downloads or new signups do not measure the true value delivered to the customer but rather a quantity which does not indicate the level of customer satisfaction with the product or service.

More time or money users spend presents more qualitative metric and here are few examples where NSM captures the value level delivered to the customer, not by any single department but the whole business:

- Facebook: monthly active users
- Airbnb: number of nights booked
- Medium: total time spent reading
- Amazon: Number of Prime members' purchases

When adopting this method, the whole organization from marketing, sales, customer service, fulfillment, purchasing and so on work towards the single common goal. Measuring this type of KPI becomes much more meaningful, it brings the whole organization together in the effort for a long-term growth, while at the same time ensures the best customer experience.

Rolling Out

Once the plan is agreed and laid out, the main focus in rollouts is delivery on the planned process. Individual and team responsibilities are clear and their reward should depend on success of the implementation.

The focus is on business change - not on Social Media and the selling methods. Many organizations make the mistake of treating social selling as a channel specific matter (i.e. Instagram, YouTube, Facebook, Twitter, etc.) while the real emphasis is on the new way you connect and do business with potential clients. The change process must be effectively managed with clear responsibilities explained to all. Sometimes, the organization will have to adapt roles and even reporting structures.

Testing and Measuring

Test, Measure, Learn and Improve. No matter how well planned, and simplified your process is, it is extremely important to stay agile and be able to make change on the move.

A good example is found in various algorithms that all social media and search angine providers use. It is known that they are in constant change and improvement, so should your process also be. Google, for example, changes its algorithms 500 – 600 times a year. Similarly, Social Media channels release hundreds of changes every year. LinkedIn is no different and their algorithms, user interface, features, tools, and options change continuously.

The content and blog posts that attracted thousands of views, shares, and likes at one point in time, may only get few at the other. The only way to ensure you are on top of the game is to keep testing, measuring and adapting. In recent months, posts with native video (video not shared by a link from let's say YouTube, but those which are uploaded directly to LinkedIn) are favored over some text formats. But at the same time, the 'short form' (status or post) tends to get more views, likes, comments, and shares than the 'long form' (articles). This is partially because the short form is quicker to consume than long form and therefore attracts more user interest.

Social Media in general with LinkedIn no exception, is all about engagement and whichever content gets more views and member's interaction will always be favored.

LINKEDIN SETUP

Profile

The profile is the basis of your LinkedIn presence and for all other activities which we will be covering in this part of the book. It is the reflection of your personal and business brand which in effect will be the foundation of your LinkedIn existence and all the activities which you will engage in.

Let's presume that your goal is to attract potential clients for your consultancy services, then positioning yourself as the industry expert with portfolio of articles, posts on business strategies, images and videos on best practices and case studies, links and references to other content, website or other influencers will help you to achieve authoritative voice. Professional qualifications, past performance, tangible results and links to other prominent industry names will substantiate your brand and help you build thought leadership in your designated sector.

What's most important to remember however is your potential target market and what is in there for them! No matter how good your personal branding, experience, education or photo is, a potential client will ask: Are you a domain expert? What makes you different to other specialists in the sector? What is the pain you cure and more specifically, how can you help me?

Just as an example, adding a professional photo to your profile makes you 14x more likely to be found on LinkedIn and will get you 21x more profile views.

Photo

Although your photo seems the most obvious thing to get right, people still get it wrong. One thing which you must keep in mind is that LinkedIn is a social network for professionals. Personal photos with kids, pets or from holiday are best left to other media channels such as Facebook, Instagram, SnapChat, etc.

It is not unusual that people use professional photographers to create a quality portrait photograph of themselves just for LinkedIn. But still, a decent image can also be made using a smartphone, tablet or digital camera.

Header image

It is difficult to say which image is more important, personal or the header – but the latter for sure is the one that people will spend more time looking at and will make the first impression.

What I come across daily is that users still have the default image in the background – missing a great opportunity to say more about themselves in support of their profile.

Best case examples of images to use are:

- Being on stage presenting. This immediately recognizes your leadership and professional authority.
- Being with a recognized influencer. Provides you with direct association with that person and ads to your credibility
- Being with a VIP person. It shows that you socialize in upper professional circles and meet other people of influence
- Image of the product/brand logo. This may graphically represent the product you are associated with or brand that has built an industry recognition

Name

There are few things to remember when adding your name:

- First name limit is 20 characters and Last name: 40
- Some people use their first name to add a professional title such as Professor, Dr., etc., or surname to add their qualifications/ honors (MBA, Ph.D., OBE, MBE, etc.)
- If your name is common, use the photograph to be easier recognized by those users looking for you.
- Add your middle name only if others know you by it. Better still is to just use the middle name initial

Headline

Straight below your name is the headline. This is your USP (Unique Selling Point) and what sets you apart. These are the tangible accomplishments that substantiate your expertise.

Denis Zekic

Founder of CeeDoo.com | International Speaker | Author | Award Winner | LinkedIn Expert | Social Selling Trainer

London, United Kingdom

Headline has a 120-character limit, so choose wisely what will go in there. The content you put here will in effect be the keywords that you will be found by others who search for particular professionals. i.e. if someone looks for charted accountants, this is the place to say it and be found by

Best case examples are:

- Use of short statements
- Mention any awards
- Professional Qualifications/Industry memberships
- Particular interests/areas of expertise
- I help _____ to achieve ______
- Also, you can use specific characters to split the key-phrases between them (i.e. > | ► ▌- •)

URL link

If you have a website, provide the link back to it. There are few places where you can add the link, but the most obvious one is in on the right-hand side under the "Contact and Personal Info."

You can add up to three URLs (web addresses) there, so if you have any particular landing pages, downloads, forms, a blog, etc. you can use this space for that purpose.

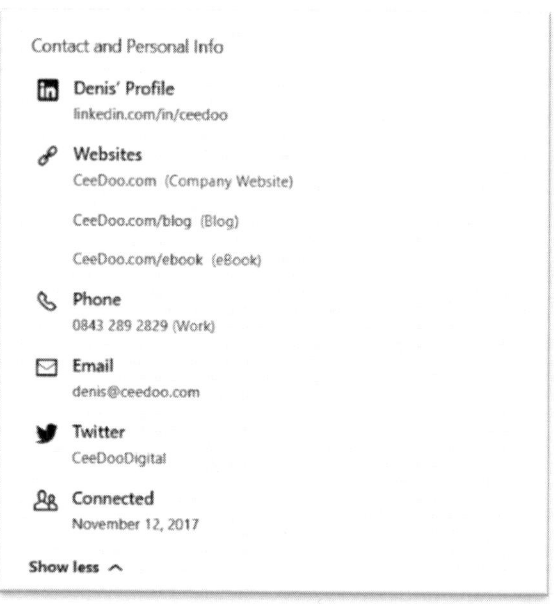

Further places are Headline, Summary, Media, Current role, and others text part of the profile. However, you must remember that adding web address in these additional places will not result in creating a hyperlink (a click-through link). The idea is to promote your brand or let others know there are specific inline locations where they can find further information or resources about your produces of services.

Contact info

For contact info, perhaps the most important is to keep it up to date and give as many options for connections to get in touch as you can. For example, I use LinkedIn as my professional address book, always there to quickly search and get to somebody.

It is useful when on a mobile device, you can quickly go to a contact and click on their phone number. Your device will dial the number automatically.

It is also useful to know, that you can add your Skype ID, Yahoo! Messenger, Google Hangouts, and few others. (At the time of writing, unfortunately, Facebook messenger was not available).

If you use Twitter, you can add your Twitter handle too. This is done in Settings & Privacy, under the Partners and services section of the Account tab.

The top option in the 'Contact and Personal Info' is your unique LinkedIn address. Make sure you make it more recognizable, for example, you can change it from something that looks like this:

linkedin.com/in/denis-zekic-330566143

to something like

linkedin.com/in/deniszekic

Summary

Think about a traditional mail order magazine advert. It has a heading, problem, solution, and call to action. (AIDA: Attention –

Interest – Desire – Action). Similarly, your LinkedIn profile must fit all these parameters.

If your heading fails to resonate with the visitor, it is less likely that they will scroll down to read more. But if the heading worked its purpose – the next heavy lifting part of your profile is the 'Summary.' The summary is perhaps the second most important part of your profile. Here, you must communicate with the visitor, address the common problems and pain you want them to identify with. If their need is not the one you described, don't waste your time - let them leave your profile, they are not your target market. Or if you believe they are, then make sure your profile addresses that.

But if you resonate with their problem, then keep digging. Give them the reason to believe that you are their rescuer and the solution you provide is the one they need. Include a link to your eBook, articles, media, images, testimonials and so on…

Experience

This is the place where you can display all your previous work, achievements and business results. Don't shy away from quantifying these in terms of revenue created, accounts opened, clients served, website visits reached, or anything else that can be measured and may substantiate the past performance.

Use bullet points to describe your qualities, solutions, credibility or list external links to websites for extra information to be checked.

Remember: People don't buy information – they buy solutions!

Play the emotional game; the bigger the pain – the stronger reaction the proposed cure is going to make!

Now, once you have them tuned to your message, let the potential customer justify their interest and validate their emotional response. The following sections of the profile will do exactly that.

Education

As the name suggests, this section is where you list your professional qualification and name the institutions where you studied.

Remember, this is where the customer is substantiating their emotional decision and if you can support with a professional qualification – even better.

If you have no specific qualifications, then leave this section empty and LinkedIn will not show it. Better to do that, then mention your third grade in clarinet, which has no real value to your prospects. Unless you are a music teacher, that is!

Recommendations

This is very valuable part of your profile so make sure you get the most out of it. Try to have at least five recent recommendations - written references from professionals you have worked with. Recommendations are an objective evidence of your qualities seen from other LinkedIn members.

Everyone agrees that referrals are the best form of leads, so make these stand out. Most of us have a recommendation written by our past and present managers and colleagues, but for lead generation, it is very important to have them provided by your clients and customers too.

There is no better referral than listening to testimonies of those who you helped before. All your potential customers are looking is confirmation of you being the right person for their need.

Media

The Media section appears at the bottom of the Summary as well as the bottom of each individual work experience. It allows you to link or upload external documents, photos, sites, videos or presentations.

Supported formats are:

- Adobe PDF (.pdf)
- Microsoft PowerPoint (.ppt/.pps/.pptx/.ppsx/.pot/.potx)
- Microsoft Word (.doc/.docx/.rtf)
- OpenOffice Presentation Document (.odp)
- OpenOffice Documents (.odt)
- Most .txt files
- .jpg/.jpeg
- .png
- .bmp
- .gif – this doesn't support animation, however the first frame will be extracted
- .tiff

The Media section is a great way to present your work, images, book covers, videos or any other piece of marketing material which can promote and provide additional credibility to your profile.

Please note:

- The file size may not exceed 300 MB.
- The maximum resolution for images in 120 megapixels.

Although videos cannot be uploaded, you can include links to YouTube, Vimeo or any other online video file you wish to promote.

Public Profile Settings

This section is hidden from the main LinkedIn navigation but has important features that need looking at. Essentially, here is where you control your profile and what is shown on search engines and other off-LinkedIn services. Viewers who aren't signed in to LinkedIn will see all or some portions of the profile depending what you set to be publicly visible.

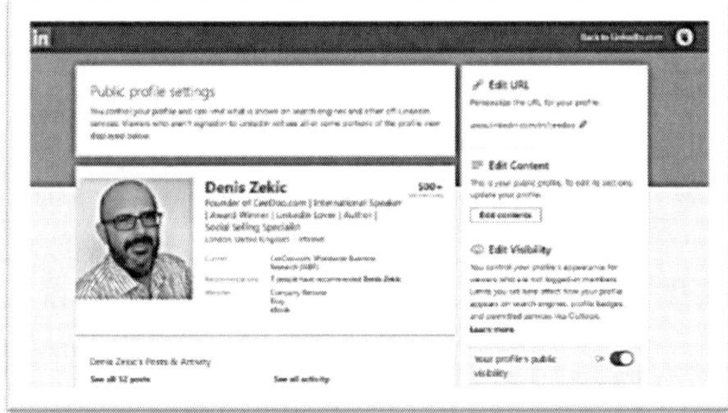

I suggest you leave most of your profile publicly visible as LinkedIn is your professional and personal brand showcase. One of the overall objectives is to promote your expertise, knowledge, and credibility – so what a better way to allow public access your information than this!

In today's world of the internet, there is a known aphorism which says that: "You are what Google says you are!" If you already are or trying to become a trusted name in your industry or geographical location, make sure you can be easily found on the internet. Look up at your name on Google and see what information the search results will bring on the first page. That is what your potential clients will see if they search for your name. Your LinkedIn profile will be amongst the top few, so it is important to make sure you do a good job of creating the winning profile.

Account and Privacy Settings

The Account Settings page summarizes your account details at the top of the page, including your headline, number of connections, and what Premium accounts you have. The Settings & Privacy page is organized into three tabs:

1. The Account tab allows you to manage your account settings, such as adding email addresses, changing your password or language, and exporting your data.
2. The Privacy tab covers all privacy and security settings related to what can be seen about you, what information can be used, and how you can make sure your account

stays secure with two-step verification.

3. The Communication tab houses your preferences for how LinkedIn and other parties can contact you, and how frequently you'd like to hear from us..

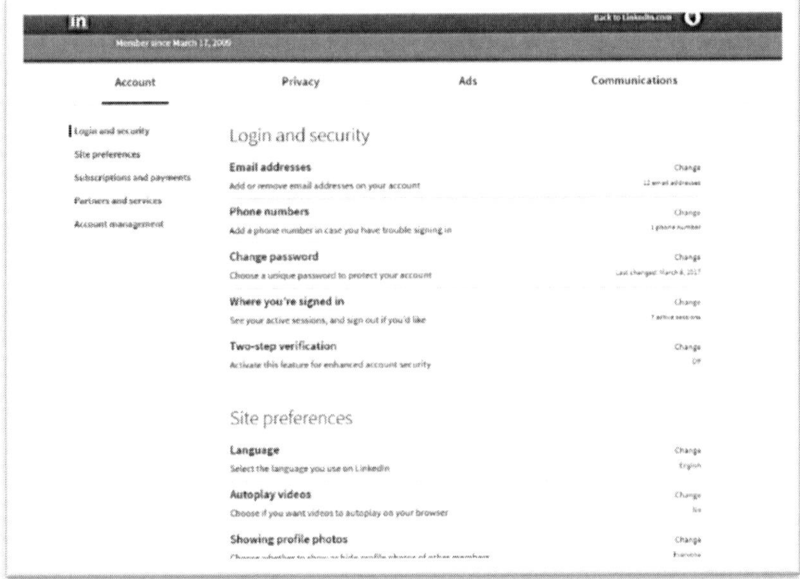

https://www.linkedin.com/psettings

Settings & Privacy page has several options for:

- Changing Your Password
- Adding or Changing Email Addresses
- Adding and Removing Mobile Phone Numbers from Your Account
- Stopping or Changing Email Notifications
- Sharing Profile Changes with Your Network
- "Who's Viewed Your Profile" - Overview and Privacy

- Turning on Two-step Verification for Improved Security

Interests

The “Interests” or “Following" section is found near the bottom of the profile and displays the Influencers, Companies, and Groups you are following. Click “See All” at the bottom of this section to view a full list.

To follow any Influencers, Companies, and Groups go to their profile and next to the name click three dots …

The drop-down menu will have the option to follow.

Items you're already following will have a Tick icon next to them in the Interests section.

Note: This section cannot be removed or hidden from your own profile.

Accomplishments

The accomplishment section lists the following options:

- Publication
- Certification
- Patent
- Course
- Project
- Honor and Award
- Test Score
- Language
- Organization

These are self-explanatory, but the more of these you provide, the more credibility your profile will have and more the potential clients can learn about your background and professional expertise.

RULES OF ENGAGEMENT

As most of the Social Media landscape is based on community and sharing information, ideas and content – LinkedIn is no different. The whole principle is to engage with others and be able to create meaningful interaction and connections with fellow members.

Those who reach hundreds of thousands or even millions of connections and followers are called 'Influencers.' Their message is read and their voice heard by most of those who will listen and read their reviews, opinion, articles, posts or videos.

In business terms, influencing others and your content to bear relevance to your target market is one of the important objectives in building the Lead Generation funnel.

You should not be intimidated by the sheer number of followers that top influencers have (e.g. Bill Gates at just under 14 million, with Richard Branson around the same). Gary Vaynerchuk, the undisputed king of Social Media across most channels famously said: "Remember, I started with zero followers too!"

In the following several sections, we will go through some basic principles how to build Social Media network of your own. By following these simple steps, it is guaranteed that you will be able to build connections and followers, and what's more - within your target market group.

The objective here is to exploit LinkedIn to reach your prospects. Leverage LinkedIn for them to start liking you. Use the platform to gain their trust. Use the interaction to exchange value, and ultimately, generate sales.

Linking

After you have sorted out your profile, the next natural thing is to start linking with other professionals and adding them to your network. Most commonly, you start with your current and most recent colleagues, but also if you are starting soon after university – contact your tutors, professors, and fellow students. The best thing about connecting with your immediate professional network is that they already know you and making meaningful interaction is obvious.

Connections on LinkedIn are split into 3 groups:

1st connections

2nd connections

3rd connections

Well, the 1st are those with whom you are directly connected and can see their feeds. 2nd tier connections are those whom our connections relate to, while 3rd are connections of connections of our 1st connections. Think of it in Facebook terms: the 1st level are our friends, 2nd are friends of our friends and 3rd friends of friends of our friends.

Perhaps you are familiar with the concept of six degrees of separation – so anyone on the planet can be connected to anyone else in just six steps. So through not more than five other people, we are effectively connected to the President of the USA, the Queen of England, Steven Spielberg or a fisherman at a remote Indonesian island.

To position your LinkedIn profile as the main Lead Generation channel, linking will be an important activity to broaden your network and build connections within your target market. It used to be common practice that you should only connect with people who you already know and have some professional connection in real life, but this practice is now mostly over. Today is quite common to send and receive connection requests from people you have never met before.

If you think about it, we all go to networking events and start a conversation with professionals who we have never met before. LinkedIn is no different, we are all open to new opportunities and having a business conversation with a new connection can only be a good thing, rather than negative.

Liking

The next objective is to have interaction with connections and ideally, be able to start liking them in terms of their profiles, posts, articles or comments they put on the platform.

LinkedIn is in many respects similar to Facebook or Instagram, where most of us share photos, stories and interesting content for everyone to see and appreciate.

LinkedIn is no different, it is a professional network, but sharing stories which are personal and sometimes loosely connected to work tend to be also popular and attract a lot of attention and interaction.

Canadian LinkedIn member Michaela Alexis, after losing her job in 2016 published a very personal and heartfelt post on LinkedIn. It then went viral and attracted over 100,000 reads with thousands of comments and likes all around the world. Six months later, Michaela was the 3rd most viewed profile on LinkedIn which opened many doors of opportunity and enabled her to start brand new business on her own.

Nothing can beat being personal and showing your human side. Having unique content that others can like and interact with is the gold dust which is not too hard to master.

Commenting

The next section talks about creating the right content for perfect engagement, but an important activity which interlinks with it is consuming other creators content and finding the right method of interaction.

The most common way is 'commenting' on posts and articles you find of interest and have your own opinion to support or question someone's view on a particular topic. For example, I wrote an article about Donald Trump's pre-election campaign from the marketer's viewpoint, which had a lot of interest, but as you might guess, a few opposing views too. (https://goo.gl/fSF7yP)

It is quite a common practice, not just in journalism but also on Social Media, to create controversial pieces of content as it may serve few objectives. One, it will create more engaging debates, which will bring more visits to your content and provide additional interest to your profile.

Remember, that every comment from either 1st, 2nd or 3rd connection is shared with their network which makes it more likely that their connections will be intrigued to check out the content and hopefully visit your post or article.

It is not just comments that will be distributed through various networks of those who interact, but also – you should leave comments to others. It is a common practice, that once you make a comment or two on someone else's post, they will do the same for you in return.

And importantly, LinkedIn algorithms also favor content with more comments and interaction so their propensity to become viral increases.

Creating

According to 2016 figures, LinkedIn had 3 million unique article writers on its platform, creating 160 thousand articles per week. Today, LinkedIn is the world's number one social media platform for business professionals with over 550 million users globally. One of the biggest LinkedIn assets is not just provision of compelling and relevant content for corporate executives and recruitment managers but also being a platform to promote the voice of professionals from every sector, industry or rank. You included.

In October 2012 LinkedIn launched the Influencer program, allowing selected "thought leaders" to share content, ideas, and experiences with other users. Originally it was an invite-only group, exclusive to very few business minds, such as Richard Branson (Founder, Virgin Group), Bill Gates (Co-chair, Bill & Melinda Gates Foundation), Mohamed El-Erian (Chief Economic Advisor, Allianz), Justin Trudeau (Prime Minister of Canada), Ian Bremmer (President, Eurasia Group) and several others.

But then, in 2014 LinkedIn released their Top Voices list. In 2017 it was split into several categories: Technology, Education, Management, Marketing & Social Media, Healthcare, Economy & Finance, Retail, VC & Entrepreneurship, and the list highlights all those who promoted the platform and engaged in conversation, posted unique content whether through text or video, provided original articles out of thousands published every week, provoked tens of thousands of comments and instigated millions of likes and shares.

Posting

In today's world of digital and social media, your content is your currency; the time, attention and interest earned from others provide its true market value. Content with no views, likes or comments, no matter how well written, educational or scientific it may be, has no real value. The objective of Social media content is to engage, inspire and create a response.

Here are few ways to post on LinkedIn:

- Status
- Article
- Images
- Video
- Comments

Commonly, written content is in either 'short' or 'long' form. A status (also called 'post' or 'update') has a maximum of 1,300 characters and is considered a short form.

Articles allow members to write an in-depth text about their area of expertise, professional experiences, personal and business opportunities, commentary on latest trends in their industry, etc. Articles are typically longer than posts, can include images and videos, and have no limits on word count (though the best-received articles usually fall between 400 and 1,200 words).

Your video posted on January 3, 2018 (1,334 comments, 25,715 likes)

1,091,285 views

2,363 people from Amazon viewed your video	
Microsoft	2,317
IBM	1,832
Oracle	1,753
EY	1,745
Apple	1,704
PwC	1,687
Accenture	1,398
Wells Fargo	1,371

133,164 people who have the title Salesperson viewed your video	
CEO / Executive Director	44,500
Project Manager	30,281
Operations Specialist	27,540
Business / Corporate Strategist	25,643
Software Developer	19,045
Business Owner	19,029
Technology Manager	18,726

56,535 people viewed your video from Greater New York City Area	
Greater Chicago Area	34,763
San Francisco Bay Area	30,110
London, United Kingdom	29,435
Dallas/Fort Worth Area	25,884
Greater Boston Area	25,731
Greater Los Angeles Area	19,643
Greater Atlanta Area	19,467
Washington D.C. Metro Area	18,754

Once published, posts and articles will be broadcast to your connections' feeds on their LinkedIn homepage and sometimes through notifications. If they like or comment, then their connections (your 2nd tier) will be introduced to your content and can like, share and comment too.

The best pieces of content occasionally become viral, with millions of views, thousands of likes and comments. Setting your public profile visibility to "everyone" will enable distribution of your articles publicly both on and off LinkedIn.

Messaging

LinkedIn messaging is equivalent to Facebook Messenger, or to put it even simpler, it is the platform's internal emailing system.

The basic principle to understand is that you can only send

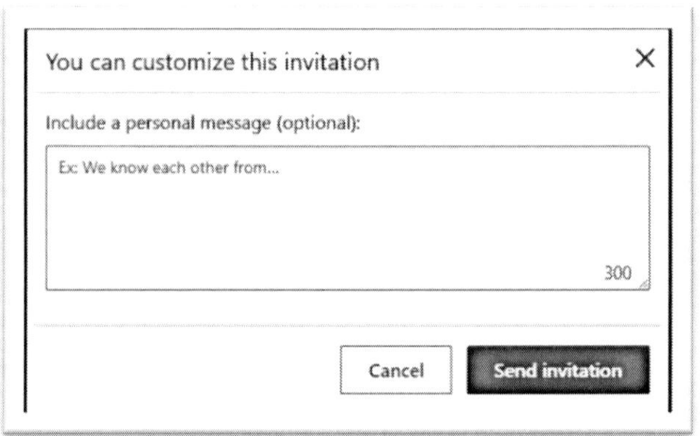

messages to your 1st contacts. If you wish to contact a 2nd or 3rd level contact, the best way is to send a connection request with a maximum of 300 characters. Once the recipient accepts your request, they in effect become your 1st connection and there is no more limitation in message size.

The other option is to use 'InMail' which is part of 'LinkedIn Premium' paid service. Depending on the subscription level, you will have included some InMail messages to send to anyone who is on LinkedIn and with no size restriction.

Additionally, you can attach multiple files to messages you send on LinkedIn. File types are:

- Documents - csv, xls, xlsx, doc, docx, ppt, pptx, pdf, txt, html, htm
- Images - gif, jpeg, jpg, png, bmp

The combined file sizes cannot exceed 2 MB.

A recently added feature in LinkedIn messaging is an option to show your connections when active on LinkedIn or available on mobile. This can be turned on and off.

What is important to mention here is that messaging is one of the most important parts of LinkedIn Lead Generation strategy. Using messaging is the best way of approaching new connections, starting a conversation or ultimately setting up a call or meet up.

For standard email, open rates have dropped to low double-digit figures, but LinkedIn messaging have much higher open rate and can be used effectively.

Although rare, you can add up to 50 people to the conversation.

Converting

Converting is the end goal. All the previous activities are part of the sales funnel which eventually leads to this stage where we must quantify the efforts and convert our prospects into leads.

Every line of your profile description, every short form or article post you have created, connection request received or sent, needs to serve this end goal: The Sales Conversion.

There are multiple ways how to achieve this, one of the most common is the creation of a sales funnel, which traditionally looks like this:

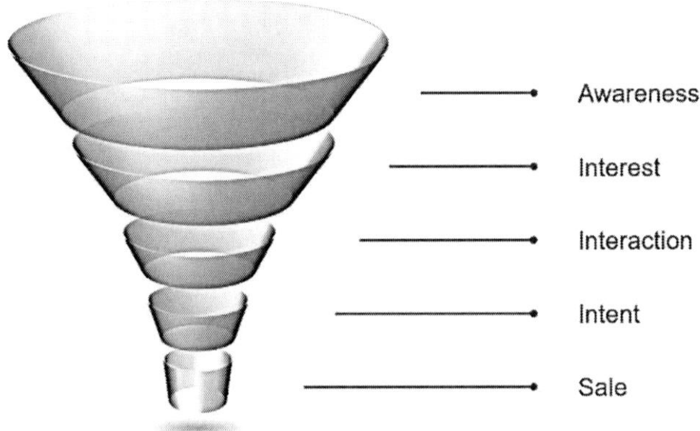

The top of the funnel is usually filled in by prospects looking for a product or service you offer. Reaching the potential audience is usually done by advertising, either in the press, specialist magazines and publications, TV, radio, search engines through either paid or organic reach. Here you are reaching out to a wide audience and expecting them to be interested in your proposition. Once you stimulate their interest, the prospects come into the sales funnel and fall further through the process to the bottom of the funnel and eventually convert.

Most recently, particularly with social platforms such as LinkedIn, the sales funnel concept has been adapted and reverted, to what is commonly referred to as ABM (Account Based Marketing).

Social Sales & Marketing Funnel

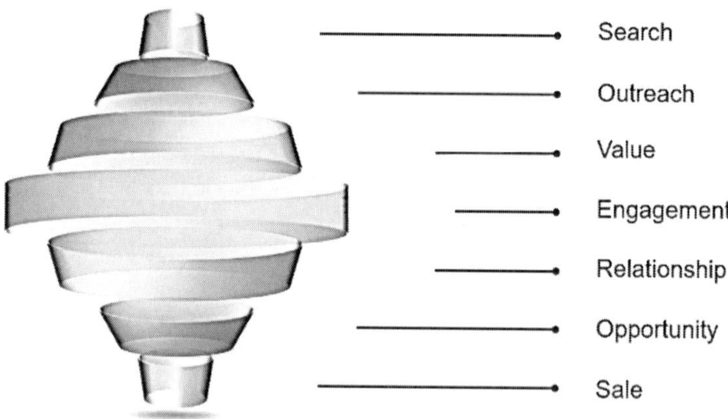

With this method, we know our prospect in advance and can target them using a number of ways:

- Active engagement via Social Media
- Targeted advertising

- Outbound marketing

One of the great advantages of social media is that you can create very targeted paid or organic marketing campaigns with very specific individuals in mind. A good examples are provided by Facebook and LinkedIn advertising platforms where you can:

- Run ABM with a specific Account Targeting
- Re-engage your website visitors with Website Retargeting
- Use email lists for Contact Targeting

Once you attract and engage with the prospect, the common practice then is to have a conversion mechanism such as:

- Newsletter signup
- eBook download
- White paper download
- Webinar signup
- Service trials
- Seminar booking
- Product or service purchase

This book teaches you the proven method of engagement using social media, in particular – LinkedIn. With the fact that 4 out of 5 business decision makers are LinkedIn members, then it makes perfect sense to use this platform as the most suitable social sales and marketing lead generation channel.

Let's now look at the Five Step Methodology which I have established as the foundation for my Magic 5 Formula.

THE MAGIC 5 FORMULA™

Once you have comprehended the key principles of using LinkedIn as your main lead generation channel, let's quickly recap what are those necessary blocks required to move on to the final part of this book – **The Magic 5 Formula** (M5F) – a simple, easy to follow, step-by-step process for creating your winning LinkedIn sales funnel and lead generation machine.

So, by this stage you should have completed the following:

1. Set the objectives
2. Create a plan
3. Define Target Market
4. Set up the winning Profile
5. Understand the main principles of Social Engagement

Magic 5 Formula is well tested and designed 5 Step Methodology, deploying a simple rule of 5's. It splits processes into five groups making the overall administration very easy to follow and manage.

The next five chapters will teach you how to:

- Search for the ideal connection
- Outreach to them
- Interact
- Offer value
- Convert to sale

Positioning

Positioning is the first step in the Magic 5 Step methodology. It is partially what is covered in the **LinkedIn Setup** chapter (pg. 83) where we looked at positioning yourself as the industry expert, influencer and thought leader through the Profile setup.

However, the essence of any successful social media campaign is going to be based on the content and the engagement.

Please refer to the respective chapters: Content (pg. 127), and Engaging (pg. 124).

Becoming a thought leader means gaining the trust of others who expect you to know a great deal about your industry. Obtaining credentials involves systematic sharing of your knowledge and experience in the chosen field. Your social followers and connections will expect you to provide expert thought and insight into the solutions for their problems and needs.

There is by no means a quick route in conquering these objectives and expect lots of trial and error. However, through consistent and methodical process, you will most certainly master this step and start delivering desired results.

Prospecting

This is the step step in the 5 Formula Lead Generation process. So how do you search for your ideal connection? Remembering that at this stage we only talk about potential connections, as it is never guaranteed that they will accept our requests. However, by using our tested and proven method, the odds of being accepted are high and it certain instances described later, we expect to reach up to 90% acceptance success rate.

To search for the prospects, use the LinkedIn search at the top left:

If you identified that, for example, you will be targeting business owners, then just type in the search: Business Owner (As shown in the picture above).

After that, you can choose if you are looking for People, Jobs, Content, Companies, Organisations and so on. For the advanced filter options, click "All Filters" link at the far right as shown in the image above. Then, these are the full options:

All people filters

First name

Last name

Title

Business Owner

Company

School

Connections

☐ 1st
☑ 2nd
☑ 3rd+

Connections of

Add connection of

Locations

Add a location

☐ United States
☐ United Kingdom
☑ London, United Kingdom
☐ Netherlands
☐ Canada

Current companies

Add a company

☐ Microsoft
☐ Amazon
☐ ACN
☐ Forever Living Products (UK) Ltd
☐ Keller Williams Realty, Inc.

Past companies

Add a company

☐ IBM
☐ Microsoft
☐ Hewlett Packard Enterprise
☐ Accenture
☐ PwC

Industries

Add an industry

☐ Internet
☐ Information Technology and Services
☐ Marketing and Advertising
☐ Management Consulting
☐ Financial Services

Profile language

☐ English
☐ Spanish
☐ French
☐ German
☐ Portuguese

Nonprofit interests

☐ Skilled Volunteering
☐ Board Service

Schools

Add a school

☐ University of Phoenix
☐ The Open University
☐ University of Amsterdam
☐ Copenhagen Business School
☐ FGV - Fundação Getulio Vargas

For our purpose here, let's say I am looking for Business owners in London, who are in my 2nd and 3rd connection. I can choose several other options (see image below), but for now – we can leave that open to all companies, industries, languages, etc.

The result will look as follows:

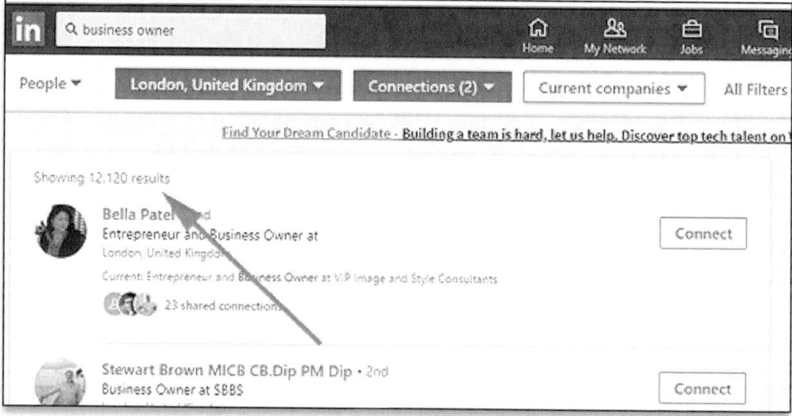

As you can see, I have 12,120 results where the title of the person includes the phrase "Business Owner."

For your particular needs, you can amend that to include the keywords such as: 'CEO,' 'Founder,' 'Director,' 'Manager,' 'Procurement,' 'Purchasing,' 'Marketing' and so on.

If you are operating a specific geographical area, you can add your local city(ies) in the filter, and it will bring only the people in that region. So let's say I am interested in business owners in Manchester, England:

Locations
Manche
Manchester, United Kingdom
Mancheral Area, India
United Kingdom
Netherlands
Canada
Current companies
Add a company
Forever Living Products
ACN
Lloyds Banking Group
Deutsche Bank
HSBC

The results will look like this:

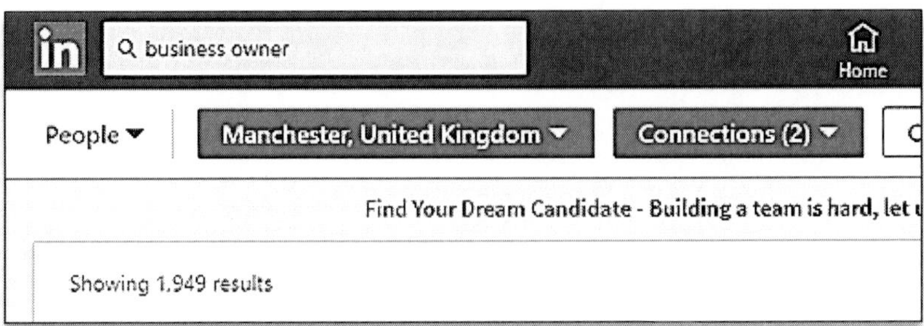

If you operate in more than one city or town, you can add more than one in the search.

For those engaging in ABM (account-based marketing) and wish to target specific companies, then you can add the company name in the search with certain executives in that organization. For example, I am looking for IBM Directors in New York and Washington DC:

First name

Last name

Title

Director

Company

School

Connections

☐ 1st

☑ 2nd

☑ 3rd+

Connections of

Add connection of

Locations

Add a location

☑ Washington D.C. Metro Area

☑ Greater New York City Area

☐ United States

☐ United Kingdom

☐ Raleigh-Durham, North Carolina Area

☐ Slovak Republic

Current companies

Add a company

☑ IBM

☐ ACN

☐ Amway

☐ JPMorgan Chase & Co.

☐ Self-Employed

Connecting

Once you have created the search and got the results, you are ready to connect.

It's a good idea to first visit the profile page of the particular person for two important reasons:

1. Check whether the person is the right fit for your goals
2. They will be able to see if you have visited their profile before asking to connect with them

The second reason is important because if you don't look their profile and later in the personal message you say you did, it will be obvious that you are not genuine and the chance of your request being accepted is considerably reduced.

Once you hit the connect button, you will see this popup.

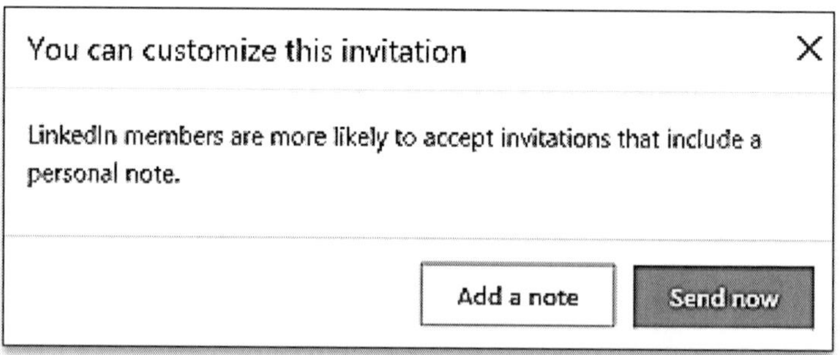

As it says in the box, LinkedIn members are more likely to accept your invitation if you include a personal note.

Including an overly salesy message at first will put your potential connection off, so the best approach is to be genuine and tactical in nurturing the prospect over time. Remember that the connection request you send can only be 300 characters long (including spaces).

Here are few message examples for you to use, that are methodically tested and work very well:

> ***Hi John,***
>
> ***I just read your article about _______ and found it really interesting. Hope you don't mind if we stay connected?***
>
> ***Many thanks,***
> ***Denis***

If you are local to the member you are targeting, then you can use the following message:

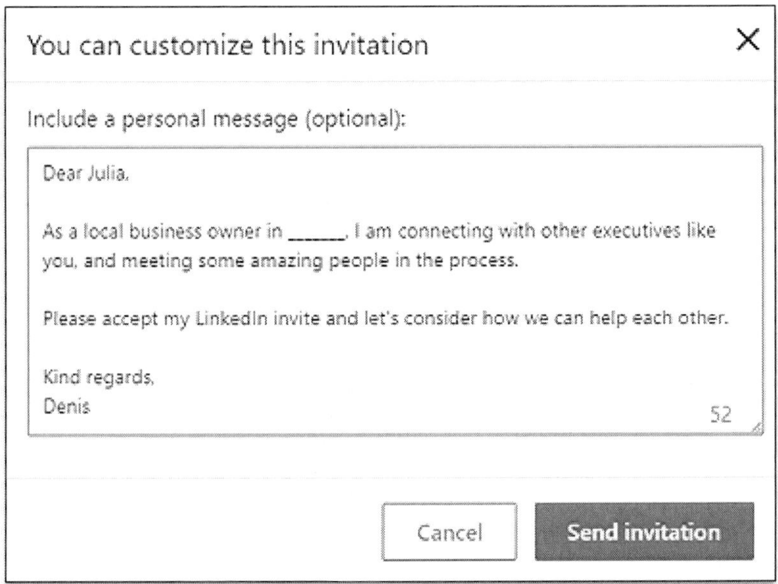

Or something like this:

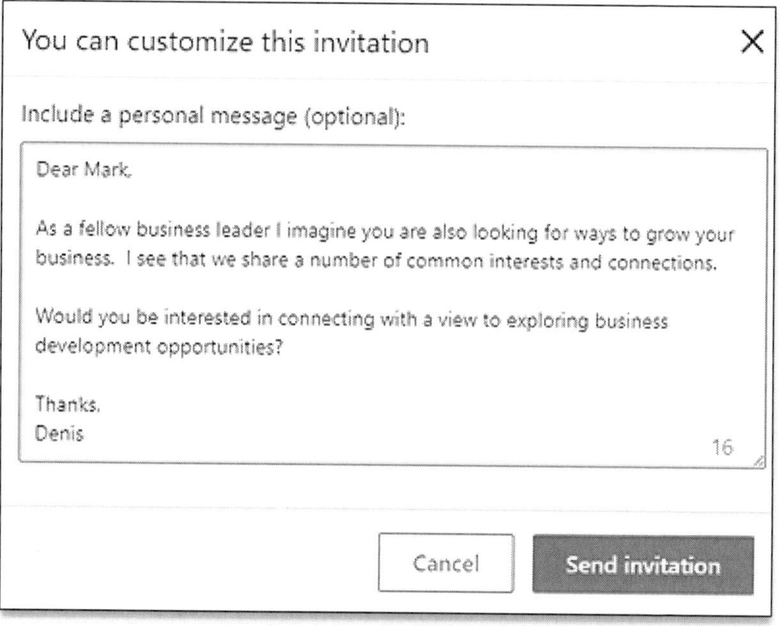
You can customize this invitation

Include a personal message (optional):

Dear Mark,

As a fellow business leader I imagine you are also looking for ways to grow your business. I see that we share a number of common interests and connections.

Would you be interested in connecting with a view to exploring business development opportunities?

Thanks,
Denis

16

If you are connecting to members who have liked or commented on your posts or article, then you can use this message:

Hi [first name],

Many thanks for [liking / commenting on] my recent post. Hope we can stay connected.

All the best,
[your name]

This example is a two-step process, but is highly effective as it involves a third person who acts as a referral:

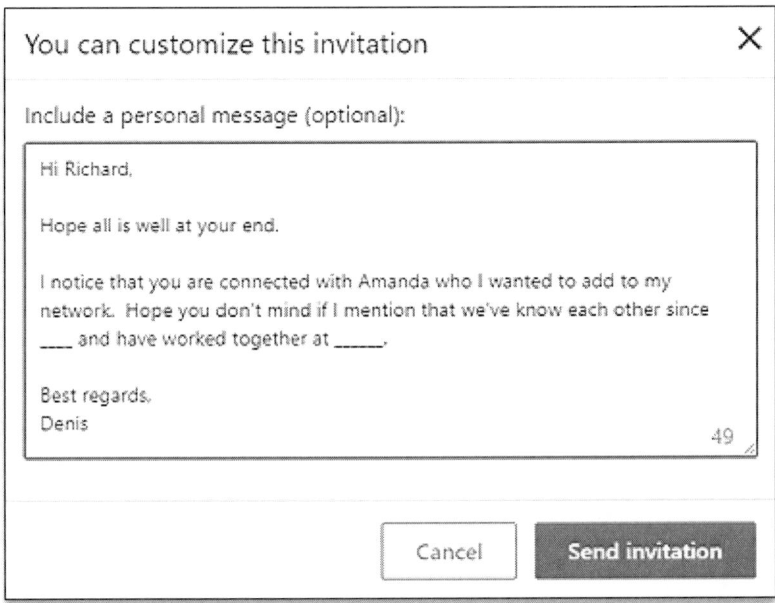

Then, depending on Richard's response (which most likely will be positive), you can send this message to the person you want to connect with:

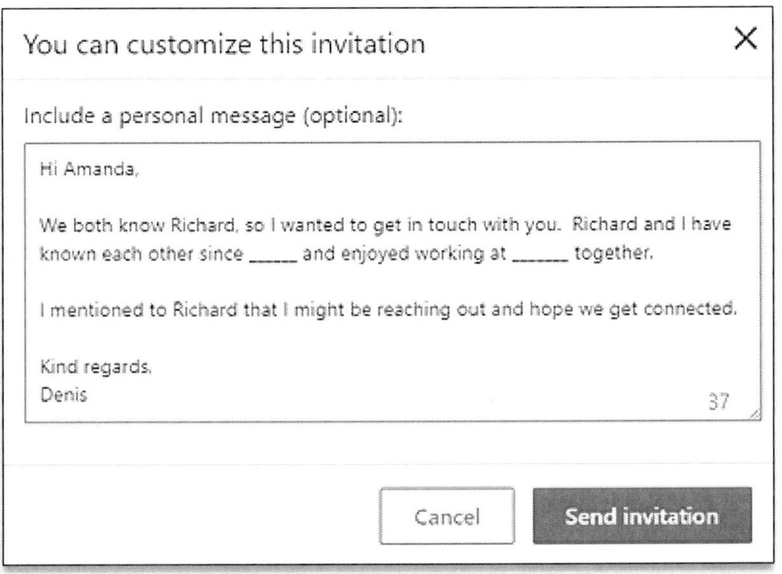

Once you sent the invitations, your second step is completed. The next is communication and interaction.

Engaging

Now, after you have received the prospect's response, sometimes, they will reply and include a message. Common replies look something like: ***"Hi, thanks for connecting, can you please let me know how did you find me and is there anything I can help you with?"***

In both cases, your response will be similar and the purpose at this stage is to introduce yourself and build rapport.

We covered the importance of this in the "Rules of Engagement" chapter, but this is genuinely a good sign. The other member is indicating that they will listen and learn more about you.

It is still early to go with the sales pitch, but nothing is stopping you to test different ways. One I recommend is to inform and guide to some additional and valuable content.

Example message:

> ***"Thank you for connecting. I'm reaching out to entrepreneurs like yourself to explore business and financial opportunities I've been working on recently. Hope you'll be open to discussion.***
>
> ***Regards,***
> ***Denis"***

Remember that now you don't have the limitation of 300 characters as you had with the introduction message. But still, don't overload the recipient with too much information, web addresses, attachments, etc. Social media is all about communication, exchanging ideas and is very much a two-way flow. Once the other person shows interest in your content, then feed them back with more information.

The next example is one where you must check the connections recent activities and learn a bit more about them beforehand. Showing interest in their work will help you build rapport and open the door for further communication:

> ***Hi [first name],***
>
> ***Thank you for connecting. I've really enjoyed reading your article about _________ which is rather thought-provoking. I'd love to keep in touch and learn more about your work.***
>
> ***Kind regards,***
> ***[your name]***

Here is another one:

> ***Hi [first name],***
>
> ***Many thanks for accepting my connection request. You may like to know that I've just posted an article about ______ which I believe is one of your areas of interest [expertise]. Hope you find a couple of minutes to read, I would be delighted to hear your feedback.***
>
> ***Many thanks,***
> ***[your name]***

There are many instances where we cannot predict the response from the person you asked to connect, and you must play it 'by ear' and send an unscripted response. As long as you understand that relationship comes first with your urge to sell after that, then you will be fine.

What you can also have ready is a landing page where you can send your new connection to learn more about you and your business.

Converting

The last step in the 5 Step Methodology is converting and can be executed in various ways. Depending on the previous step and the level of engagement, converting may include having a telephone conversation or meeting in person, followed by a proposal and sale.

Converting presents the last step in the Social Selling funnel process and is the end of the cycle.

SOCIAL CONTENT

Social Content comes in various forms. Most common are:

- Post / Status
- Article
- Image
- Video
- Comments
- Landing page
- inMail

Post or status are regarded as 'short form' which appears on the home screen and has a limit of 1,300 characters. Posts are very popular and some can become viral, reaching tens of thousands of members and million views. Here is an example of one of my video posts which went viral and attracted over 1 million views, 1,300+ comments, and 25,000+ likes.

Your video posted on January 3, 2018 (1,334 comments, 25,725 likes)

1,091,084 views

2,363 people from Amazon viewed your video

Company	Views
Microsoft	2,317
IBM	1,832
Oracle	1,753
EY	1,745
Apple	1,704
PwC	1,687
Accenture	1,398
Wells Fargo	1,371

133,157 people who have the title Salesperson viewed your video

Title	Views
CEO / Executive Director	44,497
Project Manager	30,279
Operations Specialist	27,538
Business / Corporate Strategist	25,642
Software Developer	19,045
Business Owner	19,028
Technology Manager	18,725

56,532 people viewed your video from Greater New York City Area

Location	Views
Greater Chicago Area	34,754
San Francisco Bay Area	30,107
London, United Kingdom	29,434
Dallas/Fort Worth Area	25,882
Greater Boston Area	25,730
Greater Los Angeles Area	19,642
Greater Atlanta Area	19,464
Washington D.C. Metro Area	18,752

This is not overly sophisticated but still good report which shows some basic, yet valuable information.

Based on it, you can predict who took interest in your content and then contact them. From the example above, you can easily see that the most views were from Salespeople in Greater New Your area working for Amazon. A simple search will bring particular profiles that match the criteria and then we can deploy the M5F messaging method. A simple example:

> ***Hi [first name],***
>
> ***I believe that we share a similar interest in [topic of your post] and hope we can stay connected.***
>
> ***Regards,***
> ***[your name]***

The biggest mistake when trying to connect with prominent professionals is to try appealing to their ego and say how great they are and how much you adore them and their work. Most successful people don't pay attention to groveling as there is no real benefit in it. What they care about is how to create value and for them, LinkedIn is all about connecting with credible professionals with an outlook to create new business opportunities. If you miss their way of thinking, the likelihood of your connection request being accepted is slim.

These are the messages I used. Don't forget, a connection request can only be up to 300 characters long.

> ***Hi [first name],***
>
> ***Following my article https://goo.gl/nzRJh2, I want to continue promoting prominent LinkedIn members, this time through series of short interviews.***
>
> ***Hope you'll be willing to participate, I'd love to feature you?***
>
> ***Regards,***
> ***[your name]***

For the majority of requests sent, I receive a positive response. The approach is not so much about me, but about bringing value and promoting them. These people take great care for their personal brands, so any initiative to improve them is always positive.

One thing not to forget, however, is that they still must know something about you. Even though the emphasis is on them, you should not miss the opportunity to introduce yourself. I gave the link to check out my previous work where they could learn more about me, without bragging about myself in the message. When you make a reference, the quality of your profile and content is very important, so make sure all is in order beforehand.

MAGIC 5 STACK

Magic 5 Formula consists of 5 further grouped activities forming its core stack. The principle behind this is that by following a structured process in a consistent manner, the results will be more predictable and the process management easier while the overall success guaranteed based on well tested and measured method already used by many others.

An important element of Social Selling is consistency in the way you interact with your network. To succeed on social media, you must be social and regular in communication, exchange of information, ideas and even, sharing the everyday life experiences.

By making it all structured and easy to follow, M5F has created an ideal balance of what is essential to be done regularly and maintains the most effective balance between the time required and results achieved. For the most part, you must invest about 15 minutes a day, which is little considering the outcome you will produce.

Imagine going to a networking event once a week. That will include traveling, attending the event, networking and talking with the participants, traveling back, following up via email, LinkedIn or phone and so on. A short couple of hours networking event will result in at least 4 hours of your time, if not even more. What is suggested here is that you will probably get away with 1 hour to 1.5 hours a week for the 5 Formula, but the results you will get are multiple, without even leaving your desk.

In the next 5 paragraphs, I will describe the 5 Formula process in short, simple steps. Some of these need to be performed daily (5 days/week), while a couple of them fortnightly. If you follow the process as described in this book, then your success is guaranteed. But I cannot emphasize enough the importance of persistence in implementing this method.

5 Connections with the Target Group

Frequency: Daily (at least 5 days a week)

You must research and send at least **5 connection requests** to members of your target group **every day**. By the end of the week, you should have sent 25 requests at least. The more you do, the more chance you will have to be noticed and connected with.

If you wish to maximize your lead generation efforts, you can certainly do more than 5 requests a day. There is no particular limit how many connection requests you can send per day but be careful – if you exceed more than 100, LinkedIn can consider you to be spamming and may block your account altogether.

To stay safe, I suggest you don't do more than 100 connection requests a day. If, however, you have a colleague in the same organization, nothing is stopping them to do the same for their profile. This way, you can multiply the efforts.

5 Connections with Active Members

Frequency: Daily (at least 5 days a week)

Find active bloggers, likers, and commentators and send **5 requests a day**. The reason for contacting this group is that we know they are active and is likely that they will be responsive.

One of the tricks is that you can find posts from your competitor and look at their likers and commentators. Nothing is stopping you to send a request to this group. It makes very good sense to approach competitor's connections, as they are likely to be prospects which would be good to have in your network.

In either case, just click on 'Likes' and the popup window will appear.

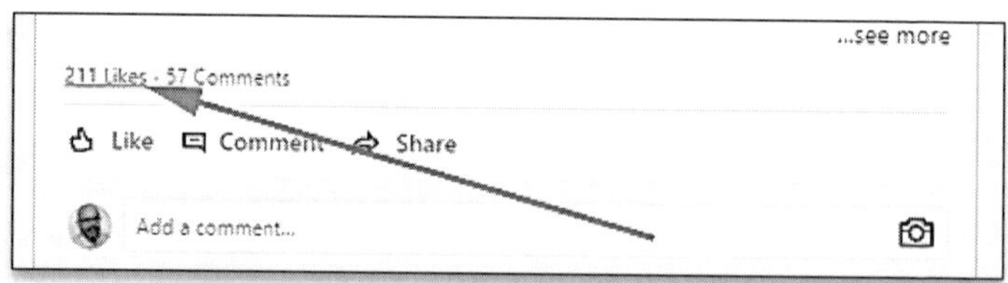

There you will have the list of all those who liked the post. Just click on their name and that will bring you to their profile page where you can learn something about them first. After that, click "Connect" button and use one of the connection request messages from the above templates, or use your own.

It is also a good idea to invite all those who liked and commented on your posts. They have already interacted with your content and are likely to accept the connection request.

5 Comments, Shares and Likes

Frequency: Daily (at least 5 days a week)

One of the most important elements of Social Selling is being social. It is all about building the relationships first! Liking, sharing, commenting is an important part of your strategy, so stay active.

Those whose content you like and share will soon notice you and are likely to exchange likes and comments. Once they like or comment on your content – their networks (which could be in tens of thousands) will be notified. So more you comment, share and like – more attention you will receive in return.

Part of the Magic 5 Formula is to find at least **5 pieces of content which you will comment on, like and share**. Make sure that the content you are engaging with is within your target market – that way you will be creating social connections with purpose.

Groups that share their content and exchange likes between them are called 'pods.' After few weeks, you will become part of one or two pods and in return, your network will start liking and commenting on your content.

Don't be too hesitant in what content you like and comment on. Whatever you feel that may resonate with you, or you feel you can add value based on your personal experience – feel free to do so. If you are reluctant, how will you expect others to do it in return? At the start, you can begin with simple 'likes,' but should soon be more confident to start leaving comments.

5 Articles and Posts

Frequency: Monthly (5 articles or posts per month)

We have covered content in the previous chapters. It can include various types, from written text to images and videos.

Creating articles is the best way to show your expertise and draw attention to those who might need your product or service. Relevant industry trends, solutions to common problems, expert know-how and so on are great types of content that can generate lots of interest and right engagement.

When creating articles, remember these two important elements:

1. Include a CTAs (call to actions) so readers can follow up further
   (e.g. "For more information please visit..." or *"please contact me for more information"* or perhaps: *"to download our eBook, please go to..."*)

2. The headline is there to draw attention, make sure it is catchy

Here are some title examples that work well:

How I Made ____ to ____

How to Create ____ To Generate ____

How to Generate More ____

How to Use ____ To Improve ____

How ____ Can Boost Your ____

How To ____ The Right Way

A Complete Guide To ____

An Ultimate Guide To ____

Beginners Guide To: ____

These titles include number [#]. For best results, replace the # sign with a number between 3 and 10

[#] Things Your ____ Never Told You

[#]____ Trends For 2019

[#] ____Every ____ Should Know

[#] Expert ____ To Try Right Now

[#] Types of ____ to Improve Your _____

[#] Questions You Should Ask Before _____

[#] Secrets To ____

[#] Proven Ways To ____

[#] Signs You Might ____

[#] Ideas To ____

[#] Trends You Need to Know About ____

[#] Best ____ To ____

[#] Facts About ____

[#] Most Effective Ways To ____

[#] Essential Steps To ____

How To ____ in [#] Easy Steps

You can also check out HubSpot's generator tool which can create a title on the go based on few keywords you enter: https://goo.gl/bUAkn3

For posts, you don't need a title, but it is equally important to make sure the first two lines are catchy, and the reader is enticed to click: "read more…"

With videos, make sure the first frame has the title included. This will be the default screen the members see before playing the video.

5 Follow-ups

Frequency: Daily (at least 5 days a week)

Follow-ups are the means by which you will start your lead nurturing through series of messages, all based on the previous communication.

The above graph shows the Engagement Cycle, from the initial prospect search to the final face to face meet up with the potential client.

There are many follow-ups messages, inMails, emails and social media messaging to mention here, but few templates can be used after the stage 3 when you have connected and want to start a further conversation.

Once your request has been accepted, you can send the following message:

> ***Hi [first name],***
>
> ***Thank you for connecting.***
>
> ***I am reaching out to successfully minded people like yourself to explore some [your services] I've been working on recently. If of interest - please let me know, I'll be delighted to explain further.***
>
> ***Kind regards, [your name]***

Or something like this:

> ***I have recently been involved in [industry] and discovered that [problem] can be [solution]... Since you are a [company position], I thought it might be of interest if I share this information with you [see attached/follow the link/download here].***
>
> ***Best regards, [your name]***

Letting them know of your latest content:

> ***Hi [first name]***
>
> ***You may like to know that I've just posted a new article about [topic] solving challenges of many present companies when it comes to [problem]. Hope you find it of interest, and please feel free to share with anyone who you think may benefit from it.***
>
> ***I look forward to hearing your feedback.***
>
> ***Best regards, [your name]***

> ***Hi [first name],***
>
> ***Thank you for liking my last post.***
>
> ***I have some additional reports and analysis about [topic] and if that's of interest, I'm more than happy to share with you.***
>
> ***Kind regards, [your name]***

When you reach the point of asking for a phone call, then you can try this message:

> ***Hi [first name]***
>
> ***I am attending [event name] at [location] and thought it might be good to meet. There will be a discussion about [topic] which I thought might be of interest to you.***
>
> ***Looking forward to hearing from you.***
>
> ***Best regards, [your name]***

Asking for a phone call or meet up:

> ***Hi [first name]***
>
> ***Many thanks for connecting. Probably like you, I'm looking for new ways to grow business and have been meeting some incredible people in the process. Would you be open to a call or grabbing a coffee sometime soon to get to know more about your businesses and see how we might be able to help each other?***
>
> ***What is the best number to reach you?***
>
> ***Best regards, [your name]***

Another one asking for a phone call or meeting:

> ***Hi [first name],***
>
> ***Although we are already connected, I realize that we don't really have a great understanding of one another's business. Would you be open to a call or grabbing a coffee sometime soon to learn more about our respective businesses and see how we might be able to help one another?***
>
> ***What date/time would suit you best, I could probably do next [e.g.Tuesday]?***
>
> ***Regards, [your name]***

If you've been connected for some time, then you can use this line:

> ***Hi [first name],***
>
> ***It's been a while since we connected, just checking in to see if there are any connections I can introduce you to or if you're looking for anything in particular which I can help with?***
>
> ***Kind regards, [your name]***

Sometimes the best way to get on the phone or meet is to ask for help:

> ***Hi [first name],***
>
> ***It's great to connect. I'm currently investigating some interesting facts about [their industry] and realized that you in that sector. Would you be open for a phone call or meet up, so you can help me with my inquiry.***
>
> ***Kind regards, [your name]***

Or, you can thank them for the connection and try to get a phone call at the same time:

> ***Hi [first name],***
>
> ***Thank you for accepting my connection request, much appreciated. As I see you are in [sector], it gives me confidence we could potentially collaborate.***
>
> ***Would you be ok if I call you to discuss my 'idea' and see if we can create a mutual business opportunity?***
>
> ***Kind regards, [your name]***

This message provides a few reasons to get in touch:

> ***Hi [first name],***
>
> ***It's great to connect with you. Here's currently what I am working on:***
>
> ***1. [topic]***
> ***2. [article]***
> ***3. [eBook]***
>
> ***Would be great to explain more, what is the best number to call you on?***
>
> ***Best regards, [your name]***

It is impossible to predict every possible message, but I hope you have a better understanding what works well and can open the doors further. The best openers are based on previous posts, articles, images or videos you shared between yourselves. Then you have a specific point of reference as an opportunity to develop further conversation and eventually start the sales process.

Sometimes, you can immediately talk about your product or service that your connection has shown interest in.

And not to forget, always test various messaging to see which one works best, and then use the one that works for you.

MAGIC 5 FORMULA MANAGEMENT

The key to success, as in many things in life and in business is consistency and perseverance.

No matter how good your product or service is unless you have a steady stream of leads converting to customers, your business will suffer. The table below shows Magic 5 Formula potential:

- **Activities:** Number of daily and monthly activities
- **Messaging:** If an average month has 21 working days then you will average 105 outreach messages to your prospects
- **Response:** From the evidence and if done right, anywhere between 50% and 90% members are expected to accept your connection or positively react to your messages
- **Talk / Meet:** Out of those who engage, 20% may want to discover more about you, your service or product
- **Proposal:** From those, you can expect up to a quarter to request a proposal from you. It depends on many other factors (suitability of your product or service to their need, price, timescale, project scope, etc.)
- **Conversion:** Out of them, let's assume 40% will place an order

In monthly terms, this means that if you follow the 5 step process every single day for a month, then you can expect to generate up to 4 customers. Depending on the annual average order value, (in this table I used $2,000 as an example of average customer value) then the annual expected turnover from this method can yield $96,000 (4 monthly customers * 12 months * av. value)

Try to change the figures, for example, if you double the daily outreach from 15 to 30, then the potential turnover jumps to $192,000

	day	week	month
Connecting with the Target Group	5		105
Connecting with Active Members	5		105
Follow-ups	5		105
Comments, Shares and Likes	5		105
Articles and Posts		1	4
messages sent	15		315
response	65%		205
want to talk / meet	20%		40
request proposal	25%		10
convert	40%		4
new monthly customers			4
Annual customer value	$2,000		
Annual revenue	$96,000.00		

A potential revenue based on Magic 5 Formula

Please note that these figures are not a guarantee but an indication of possible results if the formula is followed consistently and correctly. And despite any anticipated calculation, the key to success in any Social Sales and Marketing activity is the engagement. Being social is all about communication, sharing valuable information and ideas.

5 PILLARS OF SOCIAL SUCCESS

This book would not be complete without setting out the five main pillars of any successful Social Sales and Marketing program:

- Likability
- Relevancy
- Value
- Authority
- Relationships

Likeability

Regardless of how good your product or service is, your audience must like you. Being helpful and forthcoming is how to achieve that. We are much more likely to engage and do business with people we feel comfortable with. Be friendly, comment and like your prospects posts and content and try to build empathy with them. Liking your prospects will usually return the same feeling from their side too.

Relevancy

You must be relevant. There is no point in sharing content which your target audience has no interest in. For example, there is no much use in talking about food industry if your target market is in the automotive sector.

Also, you must make sure your message relates to your local market. No much use if you are a Financial and Tax advisor business coach in Buckinghamshire, UK is chasing freelance clients in Ohio, US. LinkedIn is good for searching and profiling your target market by geographical area, so use it and ensure you are as relevant to your prospects as you can possibly be.

Value

People will engage with you if they see value in what you provide. It can have various forms, but nevertheless, if there is no value in what you offer – almost nobody will engage. Facebook, Instagram, YouTube and many other channels usually have an entertainment value, which draws people to those social channels. Even though LinkedIn is mostly related to work and profession, this is can be very effective. There are five main reasons why members use the platform which we already covered in Fundamentals chapter: Career progression, Industry news, and information, staying in touch with business contacts, Networking and Generating Leads.

If you appeal to one of those with unique and valuable content, then probably other members will follow you and be willing to get connected.

Authority

This is the ultimate goal. Be in the position to gain trust, build an authoritative voice in your sector, become a thought leader. Those who achieve this status will naturally draw people towards them. Lead generation will transform from an outbound activity to inbound, and conversion from a prospect to paying customer will become that much easier.

One of the modern currencies of the authoritative status is so-called 'Social Proof.' A number of followers, likes, comments, and shares are one measure of that trust and popularity, where people eagerly consume your content and are willing to be informed whenever you make a new post, article, like, share or comment.

Relationships

And finally, it is all about relationship. To have any chance of success on Social Media, we must build relationships. We all strive for customer loyalty, retention, and long-lasting trust. There is a saying that if you sell something, you make a customer today; if you help someone, you make a customer for life. Those who accomplish these five pillars will most certainly be on the right path to fulfill their Social Sales and Marketing goals.

It is important to accept that everything has fundamentally changed in recent years – the way we run our businesses, our jobs and our lives. Social Sales and Marketing phenomena are here to stay and every modern organization and professional must embrace it to its full potential. This book is my small contribution to that end.

APPENDIX

Social Sales & Marketing Planning Review

This template contains a comprehensive list of questions you can use as part of your Social Sales and Marketing preparation process. Answering them will help you clarify your objectives, draw up your plan and create the strategy for your social goals.

Note: Please provide as much detail as possible. For any confidential or missing information, feel free to move on to the next question. This document will form the basis for your Social Selling & Marketing plan.

To download and print the following pages, go to:

www.CeeDoo.com/planning-review

Social S&M Review

Date:

Contact Info

Name:

Business name:

Position:

Phone:

Mobile:

Email:

Address:

Product & Services

What does your company do / sell:

How many products / services do you offer:

What makes your product / service unique:

Do you have a product producer / supplier:

Do you own any IP on you product / service:

Do you have a list of products / services you provide:

Sales

Average product / service price:

Average order value:

Average number of sales:

Turnover:

Margin:

Cost of sale:

What territories do you sell in:

Which channels do you sell on:

Special promotions:

Company

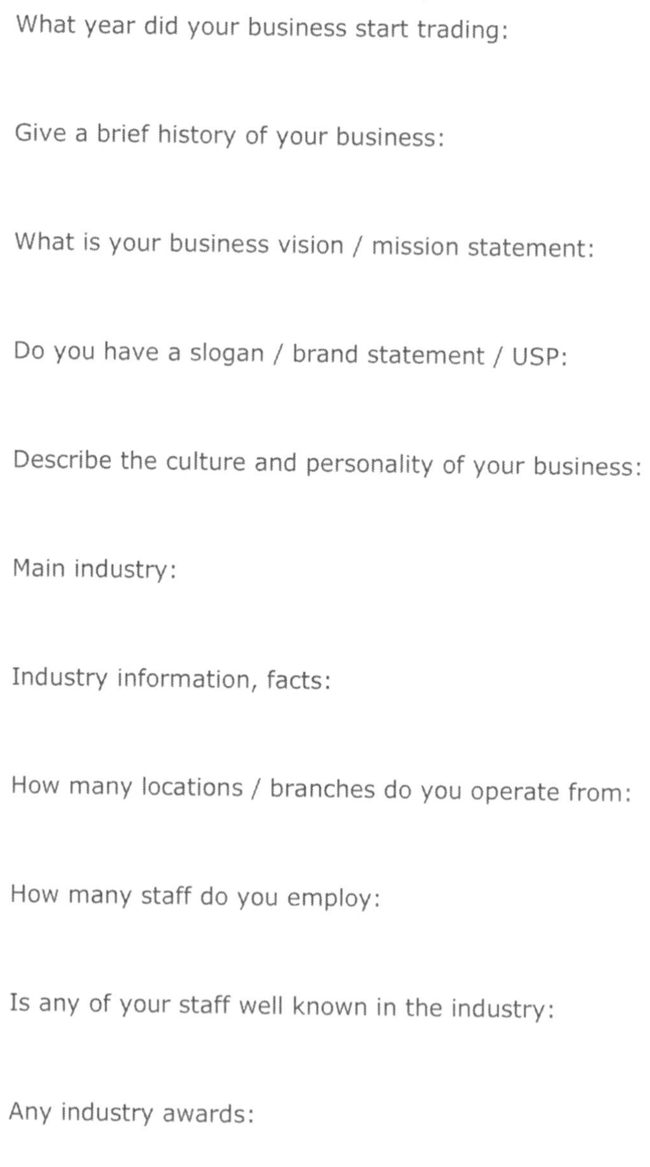

What year did your business start trading:

Give a brief history of your business:

What is your business vision / mission statement:

Do you have a slogan / brand statement / USP:

Describe the culture and personality of your business:

Main industry:

Industry information, facts:

How many locations / branches do you operate from:

How many staff do you employ:

Is any of your staff well known in the industry:

Any industry awards:

Competition

List of your competitors:

What is unique about them:

What do they do better:

What do they do worse:

What is their market position:

Do you have a role model company:

What would you like to adopt from them:

Customer

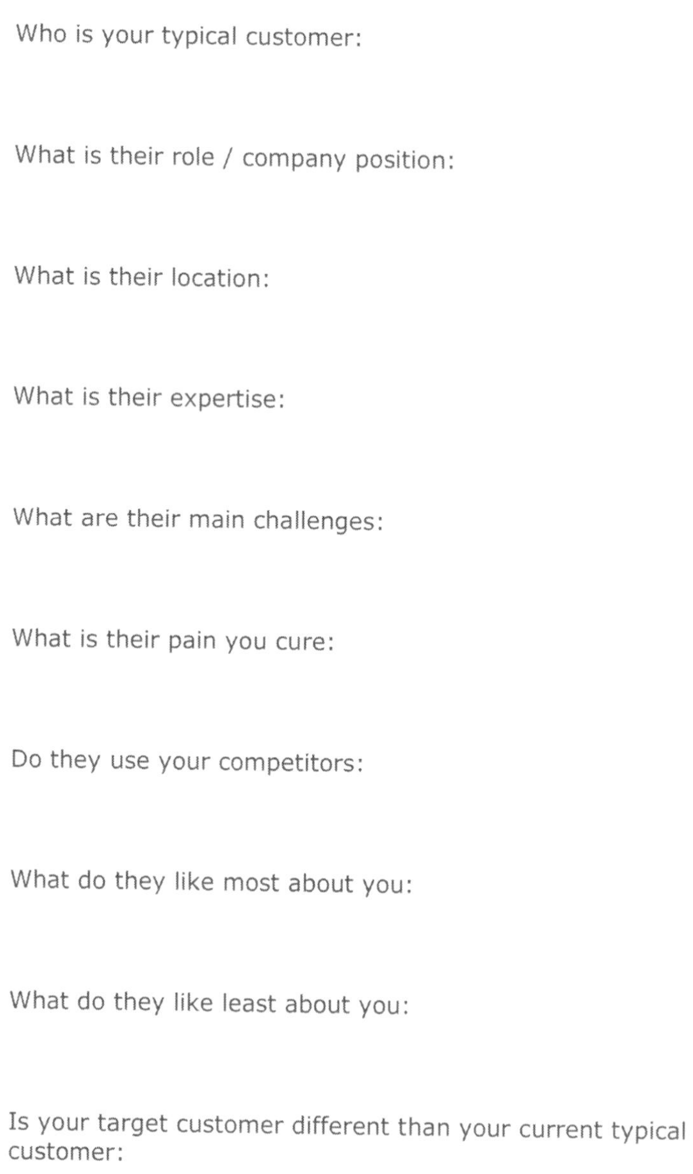

Who is your typical customer:

What is their role / company position:

What is their location:

What is their expertise:

What are their main challenges:

What is their pain you cure:

Do they use your competitors:

What do they like most about you:

What do they like least about you:

Is your target customer different than your current typical customer:

Market

What is your market size:

Do you own any of that market / what proportion:

What is your position in the market:

Any new sectors / markets which you want to enter:

Any sector / market that you want to exit:

Any new disruptors in the market:

What are the most likely disruptions in your market:

Business Objectives

What is your company vison:

Where would you like to see your business in 6 - 12 months:

Where would you like to see your business in 3 years:

What are your long-term business objectives:

Do you have an exit plan:

What must you do to reach these goals:

Do you have any KPI's / targets to meet:

Any new product / services to be added:

Marketing

Do you have a marketing plan:

What forms of marketing do you currently use:

What works best:

What doesn't work:

What would you like to try:

Do you have any marketing KPI's:

What is your Average Cost of Acquisition:

How many new customers do you acquire per month:

How many additional customers do you require per month:

Do you have a specific marketing budget in place:

Digital Marketing

What is your website address:

Do you have a blog:

How many visitors do you get per month:

Do you sell online:

Is your website mobile optimised:

Do you do SEO:

Do you do PPC:

What are the most important keywords:

Where do you rank on Google search for keywords:

What is your Average Cost of Acquisition:

What is the best traffic acquisition channel:

Digital Marketing

Do you own an email list:

How often do you send newsletters:

What CRM system do you use:

Do you segment the customer list:

Do you lead score your prospects:

What is the Average Cost of Lead:

Where do you advertise online:

Do you use lead magnets:

Do you have a mobile app:

Do you collect / publish customer testimonials:

Social Marketing

Do you have a company FB page:

Do you have a company LinkedIn page:

Do you have a company YouTube page:

Do you use any other social media channel:

How many followers / connections do you have per channel:

Do you have a Social Selling and Marketing plan:

Who owns social media marketing in your organisation:

How often do you post on social media:

Which social media channel works best for you:

Do you have a specific social media budget:

Content Marketing

Which content do you publish:

How often do you publish blogs / articles:

Do you do short form status updates:

Do you create videos:

Do you share images:

Do you publish customer testimonials:

Do you publish white papers:

Do you publish industry reports:

Do you do have any eBooks:

Who manages content in your organisation:

ISBN 978-1-98331-340-0

www.DenisZekic.com
www.magic5formula.com
info@deniszekic.com

Made in United States
North Haven, CT
14 July 2022

21322096R00093